A Year in the
Story Room

A Year in the Story Room

Ready-to-Use Programs for Children

Dawn Rochelle Roginski

An imprint of the American Library Association

CHICAGO 2014

Dawn Rochelle Roginski is currently the early childhood outreach librarian at Medina County (Ohio) District Library. She visits more than 25 preschools, daycares, and Head Start classrooms every month where she shares her love of children's books and enriches the early literacy skills of more than 600 children. Formerly, she was the children's librarian at the Chagrin Falls and Garfield Heights Branches of Cuyahoga County (Ohio) Public Library. During her ten-year career with CCPL, she conducted hundreds of storytimes for children of all ages. Roginski holds a master's degree in library and information science and a bachelor's degree in elementary education, both from Kent State University. She lives in North Royalton, Ohio, with her three children and two dogs. She enjoys regular visits to her local library and sharing the stories she finds with children.

●〜〜●

Printed in the United States of America
18 17 16 15 14   5 4 3 2 1

Extensive effort has gone into ensuring the reliability of the information in this book; however, the publisher makes no warranty, express or implied, with respect to the material contained herein.

ISBN: 978-0-8389-1179-2 (paper).

Library of Congress Cataloging-in-Publication Data

Roginski, Dawn Rochelle.
   A year in the story room : ready-to-use programs for children / Dawn Rochelle Roginski.
     pages   cm
   Includes bibliographical references and index.
   ISBN 978-0-8389-1179-2 (alk. paper)
   1. Children's libraries—Activity programs—United States. 2. Storytelling—United States. I. Title.
Z718.3.R64 2013
027.62'51—dc23
                                               2013005335

Cover design by Casey Bayer. Images © sherbet/Shutterstock, Inc.
Text design by Kim Thornton in Minon Pro and Benton Sans.

♾ This paper meets the requirements of ANSI/NISO Z39.48–1992 (Permanence of Paper).

To Mom, Dad, and Randy:
Thank you for your unwavering support and
constant encouragement, without which I may
never have pursued my passion.

To Rachel, Leah, and Alex:
Thank you for the quiet hours that you spent in my
lap listening, enjoying, and critiquing an infinite
number of picture books.

To my mentors and colleagues at CCPL:
Thank you for the many lessons taught, learned, and
carried away from the best library system in the nation.

To my newest colleagues and library family at MCDL:
Thank you for focusing on children, their early literacy,
and the purest mission of any public library: to take
stories to the children who crave them the most. I am
so fortunate to spend my days living in my dream job.
Thank you for making my dream a reality.

contents

 WEB

Supplemental materials, including flannelboard patterns, can be found online at **www.alaeditions .org/webextras**

CHAPTER 4 **Special Features** 177
An Evening Program for Every Season

`FALL`
Teddy Bear Party 178

`WINTER`
It's a Parachute Party 182

`SPRING`
Cinco de Mayo 186

`SUMMER`
Popsicles in the Park 188

introduction

PUBLIC LIBRARIES ARE FILLED WITH CHALLENGES. LIBRARIANS ENTER A workplace struggling with decreased funding, despite increasing demand for newer technology. They are expected to know the perfect book, the right website, and how a library computer opens picture files from any given digital camera. They are expected to be fluent with the latest musical groups, know how a particular movie is rated, and predict the future of DVDs. Library staff, often at minimum levels, patiently delivers these customer services with a smile.

An already busy children's librarian adds the additional responsibilities of staying current with local school assignments and accelerated reader lists, and is expected to have "that" book a teacher plans to use tomorrow. The libraries' youngest customers also demand engaging displays as well as exciting and educational programs. Preparing programs can devour the time of the most competent children's staff. Children's librarians often enter Youth Services because of the opportunity to be in storytime. Busy schedules make it extremely difficult to take the time to look through the multitude of planning books already sitting on the shelf. If only there were enough hours to plan those quality programs!

Relax, and look no further. In a single volume, *A Year in the Story Room*:

- Considers the time restraints of the entire library staff
- Provides an entire year of programming that serves a wide range of youth customers

- Allows a library youth staff to attract and retain program attendees
- Uses best practices and combines with multimedia to deliver content
- As written, will accompany the librarian into the story room day in and day out

The programs in this book have been successfully used in a library branch. They represent the best of ten years in a story room. They have been gathered together from multiple sources and the author's experiences with what "works" with groups of children. The programs are in alignment with best practices, are age appropriate, and are enjoyable for the target audience. Best of all, these programs are right here, all ready to join you in the story room. Simply gather the books and sound recordings from your shelves, print out the patterns, and be ready for those little ears, alert faces, and captivated imaginations. Have no worry that increasing your attendance will be problematic. When the children return and bring their friends, you'll be well prepared; simply turn to the next page of *A Year in the Story Room*.

Each chapter begins with a few words about the theory behind the program's design. While the programs were designed with the goal of entertaining a specific audience, they were also structured with educational theory in mind. Librarians have always conducted programs filled with books, rhymes, flannelboards, and songs. Researchers have confirmed that all those things are instrumental in preparing children to read.[1] What is done in storytime meets the criteria for developing early literacy skills. Our storytime elements do not need to change. But we do need to keep in mind the reasons we are including each book, rhyme, and song. Our knowledge gives us power. We can use that power to foster a love of reading and indirectly create readers. Preparing children for school and assuring they are ready to read are an admirable focus for all children's librarians and public libraries.

While these plans are "ready-to-go," some advance preparation is necessary. A time line to aid preparation is offered to minimize the time spent on planning. Materials and supplies, in list format, will need to be gathered or purchased in advance. The Plan Ahead section of each chapter is intended as a guide.

Follow the thumbnail links in each section to print out the patterns for the flannelboards and magnet boards. Allow enough time to finish the cutting and laminating. Sample letters to parents, rhyme sheets, and book club worksheets are ready to be printed from the appendixes and through the links provided. Shopping lists have been developed. Sources for materials have been offered but are by no means exclusive. Feel free to deviate so as to best meet an individual library's needs and budget.

Many tips and tricks for working with a particular age group are contained in each chapter. Based on experience, these suggestions are offered to help each and every storytime run smoothly. Working with children cannot be done successfully without some flexibility. Keeping this need in mind and using the ideas and approach in this book will save planning time, maximize children's enjoyment of storytime, and develop early literacy skills.

Good luck and enjoy!

NOTE

1. National Academy of Education, *Becoming a Nation of Readers: The Report of the Commission on Reading* (1985), 23.

Littlest Learners

Programming for Babies

FEW BABIES ARE WELCOME INTO THEATERS, FINE DINING ESTABLISHMENTS, or even places of worship. They cry, fuss, attract attention, and create commotion. Infants are unpredictable and unable to understand the decorum required of a library. Still, libraries advertise and recruit the youngest of babies into the library purposefully.

Librarians have good reason to draw the youngest of the community into storytime. Research demonstrates that literacy can begin even before birth. Decades ago researchers Bradley and Bryant were proving that the experiences a child has before going to school influence his school-age ability to learn.[1] According to "Becoming a Nation of Readers: Report of the Commission on Reading," "The single most important activity for building the knowledge required for eventual success in reading is reading aloud to children."[2] The Commission confirmed that the number of literate experiences a young child is exposed to directly affects the nature and extent of adult capacities.

The physical capability to read must be hardwired into the brain. While many of the processes are automatic, full development cannot be achieved without excellent caregiving. The baby's brain contains 100 billion neurons and ten times that many "glue" (*glial*) cells that protect and nourish them. Each of the billions of neurons sends out long, spindly signal senders (*axons*) to make connections to the shorter, bushier signal receivers (*dendrites*) of other neurons. Axons and dendrites create this "wiring." Sending the electrical impulse across the gap (the *synapse*) to make the connections between the cells creates the brain's communication structure. The brain first makes the networks that are required for survival. But the child's sensory experiences control not only the number of neurons but also their size and strength. A caring, stimulating environment sends more electrical impulses, creating more neurons and literally growing a bigger brain.[3]

A child's capacity to learn therefore is directly related to the number of pathways that are formed and strengthened. Talking and reading to babies help their brain neurons connect. When a connection is used repeatedly in the early years, it becomes permanent. The more experiences parents provide to their babies, the more opportunities babies have to permanently establish learning pathways in their brains. Repetition is not just something babies enjoy; it is something they need in order to learn successfully.

Library programs for babies are specifically designed to be filled with repetition. They are to be filled with activities that encourage infants to play and interact with books. Reading out loud to babies teaches that books are important and that reading is a positive experience.

While the primary intent for baby storytime may be to connect the infants' developing synapses in a fun way, the storytime is also an opportunity to model strategies that parents can use to develop early literacy skills and help create that larger brain outside of the library. Story programs can help parents provide a foundation for reading success. We can share information about early literacy with parents. But, while talking to caregivers, we must keep the focus on the baby. We must keep them engaged in fine and gross motor development and language rich activities. Together with the parents, librarians help young children on the road to a lifelong love of reading and books.

Preparation

In this chapter, a one-year plan is divided into four seasons. Each quarter offers a repetitive lineup of songs and rhymes. The variety from week to week will come from the books that are read out loud. Following each plan is a suggested book list. Both age-appropriate and seasonally appropriate titles are listed. It is possible to choose the titles to be "themed," but it is not necessary.

The books and activities are presented in the order they should be used with the children. Keeping the order of the activities the same is not only to assist the librarian but also to benefit the children. The children need to alternate between a still listening time and an active movement time. Additionally, each rhyme should be repeated several times, as we previously discussed. Rhymes and songs can be repeated more quickly, softly, loudly, or slowly to keep attention high and offer some variation for the adults. Repetition also gives the babies the opportunity to babble and sing along with a beloved verse. The entire group should clap and cheer after the completion of each and every rhyme and each book. Babies love praise, and often the "cheering time" is their first opportunity to participate in the program by clapping.

As the group assembles, ask the adults to sit in a circle on the floor of the story room with their children on their laps. A few folding chairs should be available for elderly caregivers or expectant mothers. When it is time to begin, join the circle yourself. For the rhymes, sitting on the floor along with the audience is an advantage to model the movements of each rhyme. Some presenters may feel more comfortable using a doll for modeling. Slide up to a stool or chair for the book reading so all can see the illustrations. As your babies arrive, pass out the rhyme sheets (found in appendix A, available for copying) to the adults. Before performing a rhyme, offer a brief explanation of the movements for each song or rhyme. (Another advantage to keeping the program the same for a quarter of the year is that the motions of each song and rhyme become familiar to the caregivers and less explanation is needed. By the end of the quarter, the program moves very smoothly, and even the babies know when their favorite part is coming.)

Before entering into your program it is necessary to set a few ground rules for the participants. Remind them at the start of each session that babies are not capable of perfect library behavior. Assure caregivers that you are okay with some fussing, squirming, burping, farting, spitting up, and a bit of wandering. However, be definitive on setting limits. Explain that while some crying is acceptable, when other babies join in with a fussy friend it is time to take the unhappy children outside the story room to give them a minute to regain composure. Assure caregivers that if they step out of the room, they are always welcome to rejoin the group, whether in a few minutes or at the next session. If one wanderer starts a parade of wandering babies, ask caregivers to return all children to their laps. After establishing these guidelines, tell caregivers that they will be participating with their child. Explain that the program is interactive and requires parental participation.

When the climate of story hour is set, introduce yourself and invite each caregiver to introduce herself and to share her child's name and age. Welcome each child by name, and when all attendees have been introduced start into your opening. Every storytime begins with the librarian's own unique opening. There are many ways to start a storytime. An example of an opening sequence is offered in appendix B. Whether you choose a song, puppet, or rhyme, make your opening unique. Over time children will identify the opening component of storytime with a favorite librarian. Move quickly into your hello song. Music captures attention, and the babies have already been patient throughout your housekeeping discussion and introductions.

As you move through the activities, linger and repeat favorites. Find opportunities to interject the suggested literacy statements into transition times (or use your own). Informally educate the caregivers, being careful not to lose the babies' attention while you share information. Don't alienate those adults already present by lecturing them on what they may already know, that reading is important. The children are already in the library—that is an awesome first step in raising a reader! Praise the caregivers for coming and making literacy a priority for their child.

Insert the longer of your chosen books when attention is highest. Don't be alarmed if while you read the babies start exploring the room. But keep to your previously stated limits. The babies are still being exposed to words and literature. After finishing the story, quickly move into your next rhyme. The activities that follow the books are time-tested favorites as they rein the children in, ideally back to their caregiver's lap. Music is useful in redirecting attention to the rhymes and accompanying movements. If necessary, specifically request that parents bring babies back to their laps for a bouncing, singing, or clapping rhyme.

After listening to two stories and participating in approximately eight rhyming activities, most infants have reached their saturation point. It is time to excite them with a new visual activity. Blow bubbles slowly during the bubble song. Walk around the circle, being sure to blow bubbles near each child. Stationary babies will track the bubbles with their eyes if you blow them several inches above their line of vision. Blow some bubbles up high, some at eye level, and some toward the ground. Walking babies will enjoy stepping on the bubbles that remain on the floor. Bubbles may still be floating through the air as you move into the goodbye song. The babies may be more interested in the bubbles then the motions of your final song. That is okay. They are still hearing an activity that fuels their developing brain.

When the goodbye song ends, place a basket of board books and a toy set in the center of the circle. Invite the caregivers to individually share a book or two with their babies and to socialize a bit with the other families as the babies play. The librarian may be able to spend extra time in the story room, or may need to return to other duties, depending upon library rules and staffing levels at the time. Play a sound recording for the families. It provides a background that continues the focus on building a larger brain. The playtime is enjoyable for not only the babies but the caregivers as well. For some, this is their treasured time to converse with other adults. They enjoy the opportunity to compare maternity stories and to discuss their parenting successes and concerns. It is also a natural time for the adults to create relationships with similar families. Play groups often emerge from baby storytime. Hopefully these playgroups will continue to meet at and attend library programs throughout their children's early years. It is also a great time for marketing library resources and upcoming programs. Have fliers and exciting new materials displayed around the room. With little effort these materials often find their way home to families.

Plan Ahead

The purchase of a small start-up set of toys, bubbles, and board books for storytime use is necessary. Ideally library funds will be available. If not, perhaps monies can be set aside from another budget line. With administrative approval, approaching the Friends of the Library for a storytime donation is possible. For items that are used repeatedly, the small investment pays big dividends.

Six to eight weeks before your program begins, start purchasing and collecting toys. Not all toys need to be new. Keeping library policy in mind, ask for donations from staff and customers. It is often economical to shop at garage sales or resale shops. Sanitize all toys before use with library approved sanitizer. (Keep toys sanitized between uses as well.)

Toys that are economical, exciting, and educational should be considered. Keep the toys separated into groups. Rotate which group comes (one for each week of your quarter) to storytime on any given week. This keeps the toys interesting to the babies. The six groups can ideally consist of:

> Building toys—for example, Soft and Safe Building Blocks from Lakeshore Learning (www.lakeshorelearning.com)
>
> Sorting toys—for example, Color/Shape Discovery Boxes from Lakeshore Learning (www.lakeshorelearning.com)
>
> Puzzle toys—for example, Chunky Puzzles from Discount School Supply (www.discountschoolsupply.com)
>
> Fine motor toys—for example, large beads, vehicles, nesting cups, and shape sorters from DaycareAtoZ (http://daycareatoz.com)
>
> Puppets and/or instruments—If possible, borrow these from your library's floor toys or from the toddler and preschool storytime supplies that will be suggested in chapter 2.
>
> Large motor toys—for example, a crawl-through tunnel, a slide, a push mower, or several ride-on toys from Little Tikes (www.littletikes .com)

One month before your program begins, print and copy the rhyme sheets for the quarter. Order your music and consider burning the tracks onto your own storytime CD or playlist. Having the musical tracks in order on one disc or playlist will help the program run smoothly and minimize the transition time for the babies. Have the full-length CDs on display and available for checkout.

Two weeks before your program begins, finalize your opening routine. Check out the necessary books and audio recordings and confirm that your music playing device is operational.

One to two days before you present your program, reread the books and familiarize yourself with the music and movements to accompany the songs and rhymes. Review key literacy statements you hope to emphasize. Place all your resources in the story room and leave word with a colleague where the materials are—just in case!

Tips and Tricks

- Because attention is highest at first, start off with the longest book. The shortest selection should be your last. Please share books that you enjoy reading or enjoy hearing read out loud. If you are enjoying a book, it is likely the children will take notice of your enthusiasm. If you enjoy a story, the children are likely too as well.
- Smile and laugh if something goes awry. The children and parents have not seen your storytime plan. They will not notice any changes or mishaps. They see only your facial expression. Make it one of genuine enjoyment. Enjoy the children and audience. Parents are often nervous with first babies. They crave the reassurance we give them about their parenting and love the time we spend occupying their children.
- Encourage hand washing before and after the program. Supply a library-approved hand sanitizer for after playtime if it meets with library policy.
- It is helpful to have boxes of tissues available for runny noses and spit-up. Most parents come supplied with these, but extras never hurt. Caution parents on some of the more rigorous bounces. Caution them to take it slow especially if a child has just enjoyed a feeding!
- Get to know the babies' names. Babies love to hear their names, and often using their name will steer their attention back on the presenter and the program. Or it may send a shy but exploring child back to their caregiver's lap! Some librarians place name tag labels on the babies' backs. Because the labels are on the back, babies are not able to play

with or eat the name tag. If using stickers, remind parents at the end of the program to remove the tags before leaving the story room. Not only is this for baby safety, but washed and then dried stickers can become a laundry disaster.

- Observe your caregivers and know your audience. Learn as much as possible about your families. Some groups may welcome instructional guidance and information about early literacy. Other, more educated attendees may find it insulting. Never preach to your audience. They are in the library, and that demonstrates their value of reading already. Concentrate on a program that is fun and keeps them coming back.

- Try to schedule your program at times when babies are naturally awake. Ten or eleven in the morning is often a good time. For working parents, you may want to offer an evening session as well. It is fun to invite the babies to attend the program in pajamas. Some libraries even give their evening baby time a special program name to reflect the babies' attire.

- If you have children, talk about them. Interject that a book was your daughter's favorite, or share your son's favorite lap ride. Knowing you are a parent in addition to being the librarian earns parental trust. They know that you have been there and understand the ups and downs of the difficult job of parenting. They are more likely to approach you, ask for resources, and discuss their children with you as parent as opposed to librarian.

Baby and Me Program Plan: Fall

Suggested Literacy Statements

- Finger plays help infants connect words and movements.
- The number of books a child is exposed to is a predictive factor for the ease in which a child learns to read.
- Rhymes do not need to make sense to babies. They enjoy the sound of words even if the adult thinks the nonsensical words sound silly.

Opening

Song

Sound recording: track 24, "Clap Your Hands." *Baby-O!* by MaryLee Sunseri. Pacific Grove, CA: Piper Grove Music, 2005, compact disc.

- Caregivers should clap babies' hands, roll their arms around, kick their feet, and stretch their arms and legs to accompany the lyrics.

Rhyme

The itsy-bitsy spider
Climbed up the waterspout. *(walk spider fingers up baby's arm)*
Down came the rain
And washed the spider out. *(tickle baby's arm)*
Out came the sun
And dried up all the rain. *(make circle over head and sway to rhythm)*
So the itsy-bitsy spider
Climbed up the spout again. *(walk fingers up arm)*

Rhyme

(Bounce baby on knees.)
Bouncing, bouncing on my knee.
Bouncing, bouncing on my knee.
Bouncing, bouncing on my knee.
Just Baby and me.
I'll swing you high and swing you low, *(lift baby and down)*
I'll hold you close, and I won't let go. *(hug baby)*

Book 1

Barnyard Banter by Denise Fleming. New York: Holt, 1994.
- All the animals are in place on the farm—except for Goose. Children cluck, muck, mew, and coo in search of Goose.

Rhyme

(Clap baby's hands in rhythm.)
Pat-a-cake, pat-a-cake, baker's man,
Bake me a cake as fast as you can.
Roll it and pat it and mark it with a *B*, *(roll baby's hands and tickle belly)*
And put it in the oven for baby and me! *(clap baby's hands)*

Rhyme

(Tap the rhythm on baby's feet, alternating right and left foot.)
Cobbler, cobbler, mend my shoe.
Get it done by half past two.
Half past two is much too late.
Get it done by half past eight.

Book 2

Big Fat Hen by Keith Baker. San Diego, CA: Harcourt Brace, 1994.
- Hen counts to 10 with her friends and their chicks.

Rhyme

Round and round the garden, like a teddy bear,
    (gently trace finger in a circle around child's palm)
One step, two step, *(walk fingers up child's arm)*
Tickle you under there. *(tickle under chin, under arm, and on tummy)*

Rhyme

Sound recording: track 8, "Wiggles and Giggles." *Diaper Gym: Fun Activities for Babies on the Move.* Long Branch, NJ: Kimbo Educational, 1985, compact disc.
- Caregivers touch babies' hands to babies' toes, twist babies' bottoms in their lap, bounce babies on leg, clap babies' hands, help babies wave bye-bye, and help babies throw a kiss. Motions accompany lyrics.

Bubble Time

Sound recording: track 33, "Star Light/Bye 'n' Bye/ Twinkle, Twinkle Little Star." *One Elephant, Deux Éléphants* by Sharon, Lois, and Bram. Toronto: Elephant Records, 2002, compact disc.

- The librarian blows bubbles around the story room, letting the babies visually track and pop bubbles. The librarian circulates so all babies—walkers and nonwalkers—may experience the bubbles.

Goodbye Song

Sound recording: track 12, "Skinnamarink." *One Elephant, Deux Éléphants* by Sharon, Lois, and Bram. Toronto: Elephant Records, 2002, compact disc.

(Put one hand under the opposite elbow and wave,
   alternating right and left arms.)
Skinnamarink a-dink a-dink,
Skinnamarink a-do, I love you.
Skinnamarink a-dink a-dink,
Skinnamarink a-do, I love you.
   (sign I love you: *point to yourself, cross fists over heart, point to baby,*
   and repeat with reverse hand)
I love you in the morning, and in the afternoon,
   (for morning, *make low circle using arms; for* afternoon,
   move arms in front of body)
I love you in the evening, underneath the moon.
   (for evening, *move arms over head)*
Skinnamarink a-dink a-dink,
Skinnamarink a-do, I love you.

ADDITIONAL FALL BABY-TIME TITLES

Alborough, Jez. *Hug.* Cambridge, MA: Candlewick Press, 2000.

Ashman, Linda. *Babies on the Go.* San Diego, CA: Harcourt, 2003.

Brown, Margaret Wise. *Goodnight Moon.* New York: Harper & Row, 1947.

Charlip, Remy. *Sleepytime Rhyme.* New York: Greenwillow Books, 1999.

Cimarusti, Marie. *Peek-a-Moo.* New York: Dutton's Children's Books, 1998.

Ehlert, Lois. *Leaf Man.* Orlando, FL: Harcourt, 2005.

———. *Top Cat.* San Diego, CA: Harcourt Brace, 1998.

Falwell, Cathryn. *Mystery Vine.* New York: Greenwillow Books, 2009.

George, Lindsey Barrett. *That Pup!* New York: Greenwillow Books, 2011.

Hill, Eric. *Spot's Harvest.* New York: G. P. Putnam's Sons, 2010.

Hills, Ted. *Duck & Goose Find a Pumpkin.* New York: Schwartz & Wade Books, 2009.

Hubbell, Patricia. *Shaggy Dogs, Waggy Dogs.* Tarrytown, NY: Marshall Cavendish Children, 2011.

Intrater, Roberta Grobel. *Peek-a-Boo You.* New York: Scholastic, 2002.

The Lifesize Animal Counting Book. London, New York: Dorling Kindersley, 1994.

McGee, Marni. *Wake Up, Me!* New York: Simon & Schuster, 2002.

Miller, Margaret. *Boo Baby.* New York: Little Simon, 2001.

Tafuri, Nancy. *The Busy Little Squirrel.* New York: Simon & Schuster Books for Young Readers, 2007.

Titherington, Jeanne. *Pumpkin, Pumpkin.* New York: Greenwillow Books, 1986.

Yolen, Jane. *How Do Dinosaurs Love Their Cats?* New York: Blue Sky Press, 2010.

Baby and Me Program Plan: Winter

Suggested Literacy Statements

- Children enjoy repetition—and it promotes language development!
- Babies understand simple words at 8 to 9 months of age.
- Nursery rhymes are babies' first introduction to literature.

Opening

Song

Sound recording: track 9, "Say, Say Oh Baby." *Baby Games* by Priscilla A. Hegner. Long Branch, NJ: Kimbo Educational, 1987, compact disc.

   - Caregivers assist babies in clapping hands and bouncing. They help the babies shake their hands, bottoms, and feet. If desired, a kiss can be blown on the last line or caregivers can hug their children.

Rhyme

The old gray cat is sleeping, sleeping, sleeping,
The old gray cat is sleeping in the house.
The little mice are creeping, creeping, creeping,
(walk fingers up and down baby's arms and legs changing speed to be consistent with lyrics)
The little mice are creeping in the house.
The old gray cat is creeping, creeping, creeping,
(slowly walk fingers up and down baby's arms and legs)
The old gray cat is creeping in the house.
The little mice go scampering, scampering, scampering,
(quickly walk fingers up and down baby's arms and legs)
The little mice go scampering in the house.

Rhyme

Sound recording: track 64, "Head and Shoulders Baby." *Frog in the Meadow: Music, Now I'm Two!* by John Martin Feierabend. Chicago: GIA Publications, 2000, compact disc.

- Participants touch their head and shoulders and knees and ankles as song directs. Clap on each counting of 1,2,3.

Book 1

Spots, Feathers, and Curly Tails by Nancy Tafuri. New York: Greenwillow Books, 1988.

- Children are asked to guess about the identity of farm animals after looking at a visual clue.

Rhyme

Sound recording: track 4, "Had a Mule" and track 5, "Leg Over Leg." *Ride Away on Your Horses: Music, Now I'm One!* by John Martin Feierabend. Chicago: GIA Publications, 2000, compact disc.

- Caregivers bounce babies on their laps for the first three lines of "Had a Mule." On the fourth line, when the rhyme says, "Whoa," caregivers roll backward and babies gently fall onto the chest. The sound recording moves into the "Leg Over Leg" rhyme without pause. Again, caregivers bounce babies on the lap for the first three lines. On the fourth line, when the lyric says, "Whoops," caregivers lift babies up and back down.

Rhyme

Oh, the noble Duke of York,
He had ten thousand men.
He marched them up to the top of the hill, *(bounce baby up on lap)*
And marched them down again. *(bounce baby down on lap)*
And when they're up, they're up! *(raise legs up)*
And when they're down, they're down. *(lower legs)*
And when they're only halfway up, *(raise legs halfway up)*
They're neither up nor down. *(quickly legs raise up and down)*

Oh, the noble Duke of York,
He had ten thousand men.
He marched them up to the top of the hill, *(bounce baby up on lap)*
And marched them down again. *(bounce baby down on lap)*
He marched them to the left, *(gently tip baby to left)*
He marched them to the right. *(gently tip baby to right)*
He even marched them upside down—
    (roll baby onto chest as you roll backward)
Oh, what a silly sight!

Rhyme

Up, up in the sky like this, *(gently lift baby in the air)*
Down, down for a great big kiss. *(slowly bring baby down and kiss)*
Up like this, *(lift up)*
Down for a kiss. *(lower down)*
You're a special baby! *(hug and cuddle baby)*

Rhyme

These are Baby's fingers, *(tickle fingers)*
These are Baby's toes. *(tickle toes)*
This is Baby's tummy button, *(tickle belly)*
Round and round it goes!

Book 2

Wake Up, Big Barn! by Suzanne Chitwood. New York: Scholastic, 2002.
    - Rhyming text describes a farm in motion.

Rhyme

(Touch baby's face as you say rhyme.)
Cheek, chin, cheek, chin,
Cheek, chin, NOSE!
Cheek, chin, cheek, chin,
Cheek, chin, TOES!
Cheek, chin, cheek, chin,
Cheek, chin, UP BABY GOES! *(lift baby up)*

Rhyme

(Bounce baby to rhythm.)
Rickety, rickety, rocking horse,
Over the fields we go.
Rickety, rickety, rocking horse,
Giddyup, giddyup,
Whoa! *(roll backward; baby falls to chest)*

Bubble Time

Sound recording: track 10, "Rock-a-Bye Baby." *Baby Face* by Georgiana Liccione Stewart. Long Branch, NJ: Kimbo Educational, 1983, compact disc.

- The librarian blows bubbles around the story room, letting the babies visually track and pop bubbles. The librarian circulates so all babies—walkers and nonwalkers—may experience the bubbles.

Goodbye Song

Sound recording: track 20, "Say Goodbye." *Tiny Tunes: Music for the Very Young Child* by Carole Peterson. Chicago, IL: Macaroni Soup, 2005, compact disc.

- Follow song lyrics as sung. Caregivers and babies should tap their toes, nose, and shoulders. Caregivers can assist babies in waving goodbye and blowing kisses.

ADDITIONAL WINTER BABY TIME TITLES

Alborough, Jez. *Can You Jump Like a Kangaroo?* Cambridge, MA: Candlewick Press, 1996.

Asquith, Ros. *Babies.* New York: Simon & Schuster Books for Young Readers, 2003.

Broach, Elise. *Snowflake Baby.* New York: Little, Brown & Company, 2011.

Brownlow, Mike. *Bouncing Babies.* Brooklyn, NY: Ragged Bears, 2002.

Carlson, Nancy L. *How About a Hug?* New York: Viking, 2001.

Cocca-Leffler, Maryanne. *One Heart: A Valentine Counting Book.* New York: Cartwheel Books, 2009.

Denslow, Sharon Phillips. *In the Snow.* New York: Greenwillow Books, 2005.

Ehlert, Lois. *Snowballs.* San Diego, CA: Harcourt Brace, 1995.

Fox, Mem. *Time for Bed.* San Diego, CA: Harcourt Bruce Jovanovich, 1993.

Henkes, Kevin. *Oh!* New York: Greenwillow Books, 1999.

Hutchins, Pat. *Good-night, Owl!* New York: Macmillan, 1972.

Korda, Lerryn. *Millions of Snow.* Somerville, MA: Candlewick Press, 2007.

Lawrence, Michael. *Baby Loves.* New York: DK Publishing, 1999.

Martin, Bill. *Polar Bear, Polar Bear, What Do You Hear?* New York: Henry Holt, 1991.

McGhee, Alison. *Making a Friend.* New York: Atheneum Books for Young Readers, 2011.

McGuirk, Leslie. *Tucker's Valentine.* Somerville, MA: Candlewick Press, 2010.

O'Keefe, Susan Heyboer. *Love Me, Love You.* Honesdale, PA: Boyds Mills Press, 2001.

Rathmann, Peggy. *Goodnight, Gorilla.* New York: Putnam, 1994.

Siddals, Mary McKenna. *Millions of Snowflakes.* New York: Clarion Books, 1998.

Van Laan, Nancy. *Tickle Tum.* New York: Atheneum Books for Young Readers, 2001.

Watson, Wendy. *Bedtime Bunnies.* New York: Clarion Books. 2010.

Wells, Rosemary. *Red Boots.* Baby Max and Ruby series. New York: Viking, 2009.

Baby and Me Program Plan: Spring

Suggested Literacy Statements

- The most critical period for language development is between birth and 5 years of age.
- Books are a way for a baby to develop vision by focusing on objects.
- Songs have different notes for each syllable and help babies break down words into those syllables. Recognizing that words have syllables will later help a child in sounding out words they are reading.

Opening

Song

Sound recording: track 6, "Wake Up Toes." *Morning Magic* by Joanie Bartels. Van Nuys, CA: BMG Music, 1987, compact disc.

- Caregivers wiggle babies' toes, feet, legs, arms, hands, and head in succession. Invite walkers to dance during the instrumental bridge. Caregivers and nonwalkers clap along through the song's bridge.

Rhyme

Jack be nimble, *(bounce baby on knees)*
Jack be quick. *(bounce baby on knees)*
Jack jump over *(lift baby up)*
The candlestick.

Rhyme

Sound recording: track 12: "Noble Duke of York." *Wiggle and Whirl, Clap and Nap* by Sue Schnitzer. Boulder, CO: Weebee Music, 2005, compact disc.

- Caregivers bounce babies on lap. They raise babies up and halfway up as lyrics direct. They bounce babies again, then lean babies to the right and left as lyrics indicate. They bounce babies again, then roll babies back onto the chest and bring babies back to upright. Lyrics will offer direction as well.

Book 1

I Love Animals by Flora McDonnell. Cambridge, MA: Candlewick Press, 1994.

- A girl names all the animals she loves on her farm.

Rhyme

Sound recording: track 4: "Little Dicky Birds/Roly Poly." *Teach a Toddler: Playful Songs for Learning* by Priscilla A. Hegner. Long Branch, NJ: Kimbo Educational, 1985, compact disc.

- Caregivers use fingers to indicate actions of birds, bringing out two on the right, then the left. They make them disappear and reappear. They roll babies' arms up, down, in, and out as lyrics direct.

Rhyme

Mix a pancake,
Stir a pancake, *(turn babies arms as if stirring bowl)*
Pop it in the pan. *(bounce baby)*
Fry the pancake, *(bounce your knees so baby bounces quickly)*
Toss the pancake, *(lift the baby)*
Catch it if you can! *(give baby hug)*

Rhyme

The baby in the cradle goes rock, rock, rock.
　　(rock arms as if holding infant)
The clock on the dresser goes tick, tock, tock.
　　(shake pointer finger back and forth)
The rain on the window goes pat, pat, pat.
　　(tap fingers together)
Out comes the sun,
So we clap, clap, clap.
　　(raise arms in a circle over head and clap three times)

Rhyme

(Tickle each of baby's toes in turn.)
This little piggy went to market.
This little piggy stayed at home.
This little piggy had roast beef.
This little piggy had none.
And this little piggy went
"Wee wee wee!" all the way home!
　　(run fingers up knee and tickle on home*)*

Book 2

Silly Little Goose! by Nancy Tafuri. New York: Scholastic Press, 2001.

- A goose experiments with various places to make her nest.

Rhyme

(Lay baby on the back and bicycle the legs.)
Diddle, diddle, dumpling, my son John
Went to bed with his stockings on.
One shoe off, and one shoe on.
    (tap bottom of baby's feet, alternating)
Diddle, diddle, dumpling, my son John.
    (lay baby on the back and bicycle the legs)

Rhyme

Mother and Father and Uncle John *(bounce baby on knees)*
Went to town one by one. *(bounce on knees)*
Father fell off, *(lean baby to one side)*
Mother fell off, *(lean baby to other side)*
But Uncle John rode on and on. *(bounce baby sitting upright)*
Father fell off, *(lean baby to one side)*
Mother fell off, *(lean baby to other side)*
But Uncle John rode on and on and on! *(bounce baby faster)*

Bubble Time

Sound recording: track 1, "Puff the Magic Dragon." *A Child's Celebration of Song.* Redway, CA: Music for Little People, 1992, compact disc.

    - The librarian blows bubbles around the story room, allowing the babies the opportunity to visually track and pop bubbles. The librarian circulates so all babies—walkers and nonwalkers—may experience the bubbles.

Goodbye Song

Sound recording: track 18, "Mr. Sun." *Singable Songs for the Very Young* by Raffi. Cambridge, MA: Rounder, 1976, compact disc.

    - Raise arms into circle over head. Sway to rhythm. On "rain down" lower arms making fingers wiggle. Pretend to hide behind arms on "hiding behind a tree." On ending, lower arms and wiggle fingers on "please shine down on me."

ADDITIONAL SPRING BABY-TIME TITLES

Barner, Bob. *Bugs! Bugs! Bugs!* San Francisco, CA: Chronicle Books, 1999.

Brown, Ruth. *Ten Seeds.* New York: Knopf, 2001.

Church, Caroline Jayne. *Here Comes Easter!* New York: Cartwheel Books, 2010.

Degan, Bruce. *Jamberry.* New York: Harper & Row, 1983.

Dodd, Emma. *I Love Bugs!* New York: Holiday House, 2010.

Ellwand, David. *The Big Book of Beautiful Babies.* New York: Dutton Children's Books, 1995.

Fleming, Denise. *In the Small, Small Pond.* New York: Henry Holt, 1993.

———. *Mama Cat Has Three Kittens.* New York: Henry Holt, 1998.

Greenfield, Eloise. *Water, Water.* New York: HarperFestival, 1999.

Greenspun, Adele Aron. *Bunny and Me.* New York: Scholastic, 2000.

Hru, Dakari. *Tickle, Tickle.* Brookfield, CT: Roaring Brook Press, 2002.

Hulme, Joy N. *Easter Babies: A Springtime Counting Book.* New York: Sterling, 2010.

Hutchins, Pat. *The Wind Blew.* New York: Macmillan, 1974.

Locker, Thomas. *Cloud Dance.* San Diego, CA: Silver Whistle/Harcourt, 2000.

Schulman, Janet. *10 Easter Egg Hunters: A Holiday Counting Book.* New York: Alfred A. Knopf, 2010.

Seuling, Barbara. *Spring Song.* San Diego, CA: Harcourt Brace, 2001.

Shaw, Charles Green. *It Looked Like Spilt Milk.* New York: HarperCollins, 1947.

Stickland, Paul. *Big Bug, Little Bug.* New York: Scholastic, 2010.

Stiegemeyer, Julie. *Seven Little Bunnies.* Tarrytown, NY: Marshall Cavendish, 2010.

Tafuri, Nancy. *Blue Goose.* New York: Simon & Schuster Books for Young Readers, 2008.

———. *Five Little Chicks.* New York: Simon & Schuster Books for Young Readers, 2006.

———. *Have You Seen My Ducklings?* New York: Greenwillow Books, 1984.

Thompson, Lauren. *Leap Back Home to Me.* New York: Margaret K. McElderry Books, 2010.

Wallace, Nancy Elizabeth. *Planting Seeds.* Tarrytown, NY: Marshall Cavendish, 2010.

Williams, Sue. *I Went Walking.* Cambridge, MA: Candlewick Press, 1994.

Williams, Vera. *Lucky Song.* New York: Greenwillow Books, 1997.

Wilson-Max, Ken. *Lenny in the Garden.* London: Frances Lincoln Children's Books, 2009.

Wood, Don. *The Little Mouse, the Red Ripe Strawberry, and the Big Hungry Bear.* New York: Child's Play (International), 1984.

Baby and Me Program Plan: Summer

Suggested Literacy Statements

- Nursery rhymes are an opportunity for children to develop early literacy skills.
- Sharing rhymes is an easy way to "talk" to your baby.
- Babies who play with (or chew on) books are learning to be comfortable with books and reading.

Opening

Song

Sound recording: track 6, "Baby Hop." *Diaper Gym: Fun Activities for Babies on the Move.* Long Branch, NJ: Kimbo Educational, 1985, compact disc.
- Bounce in rhythm to song. Clap, tap, and bounce as lyrics indicate.

Rhyme

Sound recording: track 6, "Trot Along." *Wiggle and Whirl, Clap and Nap* by Sue Schnitzer. Boulder, CO: Weebee Music, 2005, compact disc.
- Bounce in rhythm to song. On "fall in," caregiver spreads legs apart and baby's bottom falls to floor. On "fall over," caregiver rolls backward so baby gently rolls back onto caregiver's chest.

Book 1

Grow Flower, Grow! by Lisa Bruce. (Originally titled *Fran's Flower.*) New York: Scholastic, 2001.
- Fran has found a flowerpot and is determined to grow whatever may be

inside. Her patience wears thin, and she throws the pot out and eventually discovers a surprise.

Rhyme

Ten little horses galloped into town. *(gallop baby)*
Five were black and five were brown. *(emphasize one hand, then the other)*
They galloped up, *(gallop baby up)*
They galloped down. *(gallop baby down)*
Then they galloped their way out of town. *(gallop quickly)*

Rhyme

This is the way the ladies ride—
Walk, walk, walk. *(bounce baby gently on lap)*
This is the way the gentlemen ride—
Trot, trot, trot. *(bounce baby slightly faster)*
This is the way the children ride—
Gallopy-trot, gallopy-trot. *(bounce baby quickly)*
Gallopy, gallopy, gallopy, gallop! *(bounce baby more quickly)*
All fall off! *(catch baby in your arms as baby "falls" off)*

Rhyme

One little baby rocking in a tree. *(rock arms as if holding infant)*
Two little babies splashing in the sea. *(pretend to splash)*
Three little babies crawling on the floor. *(crawl fingers on floor)*
Four little babies banging on the door. *(pretend to knock)*
Five little babies playing hide-and-seek. *(cover baby's eyes)*
Keep your eyes closed now . . . until I say . . . PEEK! *(uncover eyes)*

Rhyme

(Touch baby's body parts and tickle lightly.)
Put your finger on your nose, on your nose,
Put your finger on your nose, on your nose.
Put your finger on your nose, and see if it grows.
Put your finger on your nose, on your nose.

Put your finger on your cheek, on your cheek,
Put your finger on your cheek, on your cheek.
Put your finger on your cheek, and leave it for a week.
Put your finger on your cheek, on your cheek.

(continued)

Put your finger on your ear, on your ear,
Put your finger on your ear, on your ear.
Put your finger on your ear, and leave it for a year.
Put your finger on your ear, on your ear.

Put your finger in the air, in the air,
Put your finger in the air, in the air.
Put your finger in the air, and hold it right there.
Put your finger in the air, in the air.

Put your finger on your finger, on your finger,
Put your finger on your finger, on your finger.
Put your finger on your finger, and let it linger.
Put your finger on your finger, on your finger.

Book 2

Hooray for Fish! by Lucy Cousins. Cambridge, MA: Candlewick Press, 2005.
   - Little Fish introduces his friends in his underwater home.

Rhyme

Slowly, slowly, very slowly *(walk fingers up arm slowly)*
Creeps the garden snail.
Slowly, slowly, very slowly *(walk fingers up arm slowly)*
Up the wooden rail.
Quickly, quickly, very quickly *(run fingers up the arm quickly)*
Runs the little mouse.
Quickly, quickly, very quickly
Round about the house. *(tickle baby all over)*

Rhyme

(Bounce baby on your knees, alternating speed.)
To market, to market, to buy a fat pig.
Home again, home again, dancing a jig.
To market, to market, to buy a fat hog.
Home again, home again, jiggety-jog.
To market, to market, to buy a plum bun.
Home again, home again, market is done.

Bubble Time

Sound recording: track 20, "Pop, Pop, Pop." *Sing Gymboree: 30 Favorite Songs, Fingerplays, and Movement Activities* by Donny Becker. The Gymboree Corporation, 1991, compact disc.

- The librarian blows bubbles around the story room, letting the babies visually track and pop bubbles. The librarian circulates so all babies—walkers or nonwalkers—may experience the bubbles.

Goodbye Song

Sound recording: track 8, "Wiggles and Giggles." *Diaper Gym: Fun Activities for Babies on the Move.* Long Branch, NJ: Kimbo Educational, 1985, compact disc.

- Caregivers touch babies' hands to babies' toes, twist babies' bottoms in their lap, bounce babies on leg, clap babies' hands, help babies wave bye-bye, and help babies throw a kiss. Motions accompany lyrics.

ADDITIONAL SUMMER BABY-TIME TITLES

Apperley, Dawn. *Good Night, Sleep Tight, Little Bunnies.* New York: Scholastic, 2002.

Burns, Kate. *Jump like a Frog.* London: David & Charles Children's Books, 1999.

Butterworth, Nick. *Jasper's Beanstalk.* New York: Bradbury Press; Toronto: Maxwell Macmillan Canada; New York: Maxwell Macmillan International, 1993.

Falwell, Cathryn. *Turtle Splash! Countdown at the Pond.* New York: Greenwillow Books, 2001.

Gabriel, Ashala. *Night Night Toes: A Lift-the-Flap Story.* New York: Little Simon, 2002.

Henkes, Kevin. *Kitten's First Full Moon.* New York: Greenwillow Books, 2004.

Huff, Caroline. *Lulu's Busy Day.* New York: Walker, 2000.

Katz, Karen. *Princess Baby.* New York: Schwartz & Wade Books, 2008.

Keats, Ezra Jack. *Kitten for a Day.* New York: Four Winds Press, 1974.

Mockford, Caroline. *Cleo and Caspar.* New York: Barefoot Books, 2001.

Murphy, Mary. *Caterpillar's Wish.* New York: DK Publications, 1999.

———. *I Kissed the Baby!* Cambridge, MA: Candlewick Press, 2003.

———. *I Like It When . . .* San Diego, CA: Harcourt Brace, 1997.

Richards, Laura. *Jiggle Joggle Jee!* New York: Greenwillow Books, 2001.

Stickland, Paul. *One Bear, One Dog.* New York: Dutton Children's Books, 1997.

Walsh, Ellen Stoll. *Hop Jump.* San Diego, CA: Harcourt Brace Jovanovich, 1993.

NOTES

1. L. Bradley and P. Bryant, "Categorizing Sounds and Learning to Read: A Causal Connection," *Nature* 301 (1983): 419–21.

2. National Academy of Education, "Becoming a Nation of Readers: The Report of the Commission on Reading," National Academy of Education (1985): 23.

3. J. Madeleine Nash, "Fertile Minds," *Time,* February 3, 1997, 50–56.

Toddling into Kindergarten

Twenty-four Adaptable Themes to Capture This Audience All Year Long

CHILDREN GET READY TO READ LONG BEFORE THEY ENTER SCHOOL. THEIR early knowledge about reading and writing is labeled as "early literacy" by the experts. Much of what goes on in a quality children's program helps in developing the six early literacy skills needed to become a reader. In order to learn to read, research shows that children must have the following skills:

Narrative skill—the ability to describe events and to tell a story

Print motivation—having an interest in and the experience of enjoying books

Vocabulary—the ability to name things

Print awareness—the ability to notice print and an awareness of book-handling behaviors

Letter knowledge—the awareness that letters are everywhere and that letters have names

Phonological awareness—the ability to hear (and manipulate) the smaller sounds in words.[1]

The development of prereading skills is a process that begins in the first years of life. In some way the children's librarian becomes a child's first reading teacher! However, it is not necessary for the librarian to conduct storytime as she would a classroom. Instead the focus of a library storytime and the librarian should be on the exploration of words and books. It should remain on playing with rhymes and songs. The librarian should be a lover of words sharing her love with her audience.

Public libraries have long offered storytimes to the preschool set. Today, programs are developed for every age group. With simple substitutions, planning for toddlers (18–36 months), preschoolers (ages 3 and 4), and prekindergartners (age 5) can all be done at once. In addition to saving time, planning in this manner holds program day advantages. For example,

- Adjusting the book selections will allow your materials to be "just right" and age appropriate for the group in front of you. The attendees don't know ahead of time what you've selected. When an advertised program "groups" itself along the 2-to-5-year spectrum or an older group arrives with a large secondary audience of younger or older siblings, you can change your plan on the fly.
- If after you start presenting and you observe the group in front of you is mature for the advertised age (or more wiggly than they should be), there is no need to run to your shelves or start counting the minutes until storytime is over. Instead, you will simply choose the book that is more appropriate than originally planned.

The storytime plans that follow engage the audience in all six early literacy skills. It is not necessary to spell out what literacy skill is behind every item on each plan. The children are not interested in the why; they are interested in the doing. Talking about books and asking questions about stories are natural for children's librarians. Prereading skills are natural elements of storytime. Librarians include them without thought. Librarians know that words tell stories. Stories are in books. Books are worth sharing and discussing. Libraries are the perfect place to demonstrate the love of reading. The fact that early literacy skills are included in all the sharing is a wonderful additional benefit.

Preparation

In this chapter, a one-year plan is divided by season into quarters. Each quarter contains detailed storytimes appropriate to the calendar season. Every week, the plan assumes that three books will be read to the typical 3- or 4-year-old. However, having some of the additional titles available will allow the flexibility previously discussed. The sound recordings, flannelboards, prop stories, or finger plays are appropriate for the entire age range. Older preschoolers love the rhymes and movement even if they complain it is "babyish." If a group appears reluctant to join you in an activity, it's always fun to remind them that when they were little they did this particular rhyme. Or, challenge the children to be big kids and do a rhyme more quickly, quietly, or loudly than they did when they were "babies."

The books and activities are presented in a consistent order. Keeping the order of the activities the same is not only for the librarian's convenience but also to benefit the children. Children need to alternate between a still listening time and an active movement time. That need is built into the plans that follow.

Every storytime plan begins with the librarian's own unique opening. There are many ways to start a storytime. Whether the librarian chooses a song, puppet, or rhyme, each librarian should choose her own opening (and closing). Over time children will identify the opening and closing components of storytime with a favorite librarian. The example in appendix B was used for ten years, and the host of storytime was "Jimbo," a jack-in-the-box. Over time, I became referred to as "Jimbo" or the "bubble lady." Jimbo would "pop" into storytime whenever he heard children singing the hello song. Over the years, the hello song became referred to as "The Jimbo Song." The bubble song and the blowing of bubbles ends storytime. Each presenter should decide on an opening that is comfortable for him and can be used for a long time. It will become a personal trademark.

After the children are welcomed and seated from the opening sequence, the librarian begins reading the longest of the books. The book is followed with a rhyme or flannel activity. After sitting for the first two activities the children are ready for the first musical movement activity. The children always respond to movement and dancing. They need to stretch, wiggle, jump, and clap. After the movement the librarian needs to transition the children from moving back to a quiet listening position. The transition pieces should become familiar to the children. Repeat them twice. Their appearance in the program will prepare the children for the quiet necessary to listen to the next book. Using the same transition rhymes during the entire quarter is highly effective. Because such rhymes are short and fast, it takes repetition for the children to learn each one and the movement that accompanies it. By the end of the quarter they are comfortable with the rhyme and can do the motions without guidance. Research tells us that repetition is necessary, beneficial, and comforting for toddlers and preschoolers.[2] Therefore transition rhymes change only quarterly. After the children are seated from the transition activity, proceed to read book two and present the second flannel activity. Offer another musical activity and the second transition rhyme. If the children are still able to sit for a third book, try a short one. It is also a great time for a prop story. After the last book or prop story, it is time to close the program. Like the opening, a librarian's closing should be individual and consistent. Children will be cued that the storytime is over and the time to leave the story room has arrived. Reciting a consistent phrase that invites the children back to the library is cordial. Many librarians offer each child a hand stamp or some concrete symbol of their participation in the program.

Plan Ahead

The purchase of a small start-up set of items for storytime use is necessary. Ideally library funds will be available. If not, perhaps monies can be set aside from another budget line. With administrative approval, approaching the Friends of the Library for a storytime donation is possible. For items that are used repeatedly, the small investment pays big dividends. Purchase enough materials for twenty-four participants. If more than twenty-four children arrive for a program, repeat individual program segments so each child has a turn participating with the manipulative.

Six to eight weeks before your program begins, start purchasing and collecting the suggested items.

Monkey mitt
(including bunnies, frogs, monkeys, and *Old MacDonald* and *The Old Lady Who Swallowed a Fly* pieces)
Monkey mitts and the individual pieces can be purchased through www.puppetjungle.com/monkeymitt.htm.

Rhythm sticks
Rhythm sticks provide an easy way to incorporate rhythm and phonological awareness to storytimes! www.music123.com.

Beanbags
For purchase consider: www.k12schoolsupplies.net.
These can be made as well. Directions are at the following link: http://familycrafts.about.com/od/easysewin1/ss/beanbags.htm.

Wheels on the Bus flannelboard set
There are many patterns available to make this set, but because of the frequency of use, I recommend a durable source such as www .thefeltsource.com if finances allow.

Rhythm instruments
Check each instrument for safety before you use it. Be assured that there are no loose bells or disks that a toddler may discover. Two alternate sources for purchase are either http://store.musicfor littlepeople.com or www.music123.com.

Egg shakers

> These too can be made inexpensively with plastic Easter eggs. Put a couple of tablespoons of rice or barley in the bottom half of egg. Run a bead of hot glue along the inside edge of the top of the egg. Carefully place top on and check to be sure it's on straight and tight.

Ribbon wands

> These can be made as well. Directions are at the following link: www .instructables.com/id/How-to-make-a-ribbon-stick-for-your-junior -gymnast. Or, they can be purchased at www.esportsonline.com.

Scarves

> Peek-a-Boo rhymes with babies become more fun if the scarves are transparent such as the ones found at www.k12schoolsupplies.net.

Crocodile puppet

> www.folkmanis.com

Very Hungry Caterpillar puppet

> http://qualityeducationaltoys.guidestobuy.com/the-very-hungry -caterpillar-plush-toy-with-mini-book

Collect the props needed for the stories *What's on My Head* (p. 76) and *When This Bag Is Full* (p. 57). E-mailing a wish list to your own library staff often nets donations for many of the items. (A sample request letter can be found in appendix C.) Alternatively, your own attic, garage sales, and flea markets are inexpensive sources for finding these items. Purchase colored paper plates to use when sharing *Caps for Sale: A Tale of a Peddler, Some Monkeys, and Their Monkey Business* (p. 45). An alternative to purchasing colored plates is to buy white plates and paint them to correspond with the story.

Following the thumbnails, print out the needed patterns one month before your programs begin. If possible, laminate the magnet pieces for durability. Assemble a locking plastic storage bag labeled with the theme for each story-time. For flannelboards that are used in several themes, consider making duplicates for each bag. Doing this assures that each plastic bag is complete. Cut out twenty-four foam shapes to create the manipulative wands the children will use in "Ducks Like Rain" (p. 98) and "Snowflake, Snowflake" (p. 69).

Two weeks before your programs begin, finalize and perfect your unique opening and closing. Check out the necessary books and audio recordings, and confirm that your music playing device is operational.

One to two days before you present your program, reread the books, practice manipulating the flannel and magnet pieces, and familiarize yourself with the music and movements to accompany the audio recordings. Practice the transition rhymes. Place all your resources in the story room and leave word with a colleague where the materials are—just in case!

Tips and Tricks

- Because attention is highest at first, start off with the longest book. The shortest selection should be your last. Please share books that you enjoy reading or enjoy hearing read out loud. If you are enjoying a book, it is likely the children will take notice of your enthusiasm. If you enjoy a story, the children are likely too as well.

- Never be afraid to repeat a song or story. If the children are asking for it again, that's a great achievement. Take advantage. Likewise, if you create a flannelboard or prop that the children love, feel free to repeat it or to revisit it in subsequent weeks. The audience will not think you are being unoriginal. They will be excited to see familiar items.

- While these plans have built-in flexibility, make a conscious effort to remain flexible throughout your program. If a book isn't working, don't be afraid to paraphrase it and bring it to a close. Or, dramatically close the book and ask the children how they think the story should end. Some days, despite our best preparations, children are just wiggly to be wiggly. Don't feel pressured to read all your selected books. You may need to use additional movement activities or music. Have no worries, the children are still involved in word filled activities. And, they are having fun in a library! Story hour should never be forced. The children are in the library and we want them to return; let them guide your storytime offerings so everyone has a wonderful time.

- Smile and laugh if something goes awry. The children and parents have not seen your plan. They will not notice any changes or mishaps. They see only your facial expression. Make it one of genuine enjoyment. Enjoy the children and audience. Parents are envious of the way Children's Librarians have with children. Children are in love with the time we have to read to them. You, as the librarian, are poised to be the hero or heroine. Relish the opportunity.

Fall, Week 1

Apples & Pumpkins

Opening Activity

Book 1

It's Pumpkin Time! by Zoe Hall. New York: Scholastic, 1994.

- A sister and brother grow their own jack-o'-lantern for Halloween.

Interactive Activity: Five Little Pumpkins Flannelboard

Download full-size pattern 2.1 at alaeditions.org/webextras.

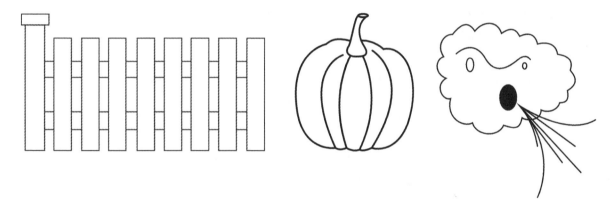

Five little pumpkins were sitting on a gate.
The first one said, "Oh my, it's getting late."
The second one said, "There are witches in the air."
The third one said, "But we don't care."
The fourth one said, "Let's run and run and run."
The fifth one said, "It's Halloween fun."
Then . . .
Ooo-ooo went the wind.
And out went the light! *(clap hands suddenly)*
And the five little pumpkins rolled out of sight.

Music & Movement

Sound recording: track 16, "Five Little Pumpkins." *Singable Songs for the Very Young* by Raffi. Cambridge, MA: Rounder, 1976, compact disc.

Transition 1: Wiggle All Around

(Follow motions described, to the tune of "Jingle Bells.")
Clap your hands, stomp your feet,
Wiggle all around.
Reach your hands high in the air,
And now let's touch the ground!
Hold your hips, hold your head,
Give yourself a hug.
Sit right down, eyes to look . . .
    (after look use a long pause to prepare for opening your next book)
It's time to read a book.

Book 2

Dappled Apples by Jan Carr. New York: Holiday House, 2001.
    - Rhyming text celebrates the best of fall.

Interactive Activity: This is Jack O'Happy Magnet Board

Download full-size pattern 2.2 at alaeditions.org/webextras.

This is Jack all happy.
This is Jack all sad.
This is Jack all silly.
This is Jack all mad.
This is Jack who's broken,
With a hole so small.
But baked into a pumpkin pie,
Is the best Jack of all.

Music & Movement

Sound recording: track 3, "Apple Tree." *Wiggle and Whirl, Clap and Nap* by Sue Schnitzer. Boulder, CO: Weebee Music, 2005, compact disc.

> Way up high in an apple tree, *(point up)*
> Two big apples smiled at me. *(put fingers on cheeks and make smile)*
> I shook that tree as hard as I could. *(pretend to shake tree)*
> Down came the apples— *(arms fall to ground)*
> Mm-mm, they were good! *(rub belly)*

Transition 2: Hands on My Head

> *(Follow motions described.)*
> My hands upon my head I'll place.
> Upon my shoulders, on my face,
> At my waist, and by my side.
> Then behind me they will hide.
> Then I'll raise them way up high,
> And let my fingers fly, fly, fly.
> Then clap, clap, clap them—
> 1—2—3!
> Sit down and see how quiet I can be. *(sit and fold hands in lap)*

Book 3

Ten Red Apples by Virginia Miller. Cambridge, MA: Candlewick Press, 2002.
   - Two bears and a kitten count the red apples from their apple orchard.

Closing Activity

ALTERNATIVE TITLES FOR APPLES AND PUMPKINS

Fleming, Denise. *Pumpkin Eye.* New York: Henry Holt & Co, 2001.

Hill, Eric. *Spot's Harvest.* New York: G. P. Putnam's Sons, 2010.

Jackson, Alison. *I Know an Old Lady Who Swallowed a Pie.* New York: Dutton Children's Books, 1997.

Mantle, Ben. *Five Little Pumpkins.* Wilton, CT: Tiger Tales, 2009.

Minor, Wendell. *Pumpkin Heads!* New York: Blue Sky Press, 2000.

Mortimer, Anne. *Pumpkin Cat.* New York: Katherine Tegen Books, 2011.

Rockwell, Anne F. *Apples and Pumpkins.* New York: Macmillan ; London: Collier Macmillan, 1989.

Thomas, Jan. *Pumpkin Trouble*. New York: Harper, 2011.

Wellington, Monica. *Apple Farmer Annie*. New York: Dutton Children's Books, 2001.

Fall, Week 2

Cats

Opening

Book 1

Kitten's First Full Moon by Kevin Henkes. New York: Greenwillow Books, 2004.
   - A kitten confuses the reflection of the moon with a bowl of milk.

Interactive Activity: Flack the Cat Flannelboard

Download pattern 2.3 at alaeditions.org/webextras.

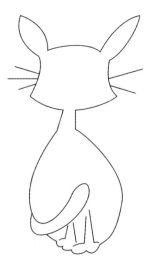

(When Flack changes color, place the next color of felt on top of the previous. Exaggerate thinking of what each color is like. Encourage the children to shout out various ideas for each color.)

Flack the cat was a black cat.
Flack was afraid he was just like every other
   ordinary cat.
So he said, *(snap your fingers)*
"I'm Flack the cat, I'm lively and fat and I can change
   my color just like that." *(clap on the word that)*
So Flack changed into a *(color)* cat.
He was as *(color)* as the *(children answer)*.
Flack enjoyed being *(color)* for a little while.
But then he got bored.
So he said, *(snap your fingers)*

"I'm Flack the cat, I'm lively and fat and I can change my color
  just like that." *(clap on the word that)*
. . . green . . .
. . . blue . . .
. . . red . . .
. . . yellow . . .
. . . orange . . .
After a while, Flack the cat was exhausted from changing his colors so
  many times.
He decided that it wasn't boring just being a black cat.
So he said, *(snap your fingers)*
"I'm Flack the cat. I'm lively and fat. AND I'm the most handsome, just like
  that." *(clap on* that *and remove all flannel cats except the original black)*

Music & Movement

Sound recording: track 9, "Alley Cat." *Monster Mash.* Del Ray Beach, FL:
Nesak International, 1995, compact disc.

  - Make a circle and prance as a cat would. Lyrics will encourage changes in
  the tempo.

Transition 1: Wiggle All Around

(Follow motions described, to the tune of "Jingle Bells.")
Clap your hands, stomp your feet,
Wiggle all around.
Reach your hands high in the air,
And now let's touch the ground!
Hold your hips, hold your head,
Give yourself a hug.
Sit right down, eyes to look . . .
    (after look use a long pause to prepare for opening your next book)
It's time to read a book.

Book 2

Where Is Little Black Kitten? by Virginia Miller. Cambridge, MA: Candlewick
Press, 2002.

  - Lift the flaps to see where Bartholomew Bear is hiding in an effort to
  prolong bedtime.

Interactive Activity: Counting Pets Flannelboard

Download pattern 2.4 at alaeditions.org/webextras.

(As you read the rhyme, place the appropriate animals on the flannelboard. If the group is small the children can help place the pieces. If age appropriate, use these pieces, after the rhyme, to practice simple addition and subtraction.)

One red dog, barking until noon.
Two yellow owls, whooo-ing at the moon.
Three green fish, swimming in the sea.
Four blue birdies, singing from their tree.
Five pink cats, looking for a mouse.
And they all live together in a very busy house.

Music & Movement

Sound recording: track 4: "Creepy Mouse/Sneaky Cat." *Sticky Bubble Gum and Other Tasty Tunes: Sing Along, Dance Along, Do Along* by Carole Peterson. United States: Macaroni Soup, 2002, compact disc.

Creepy mouse. Creepy mouse. *(crawl on hands and knees)*
And along comes a big, black cat—SCAT!
    (slowly raise both hands above you; SLAP floor)
Sneaky cat. Sneaky cat. *(crawl on hands and knees)*
Looking for a big fat mouse—POUNCE!
    (put hand to forehead to "look" around; pounce on floor)
Should we find another mouse?
    (pick up the pretend mouse by the tail, and let him go with a shooing motion)

Transition 2: Hands on My Head

(Follow motions described.)
My hands upon my head I'll place.
Upon my shoulders, on my face,
At my waist, and by my side.
Then behind me they will hide.
Then I'll raise them way up high,
And let my fingers fly, fly, fly.
Then clap, clap, clap them—
1—2—3!
Sit down and see how quiet I can be. *(sit and fold hands in lap)*

Book 3

Kitten for a Day by Ezra Jack Keats. New York: Four Winds Press, 1974.

  - A puppy joins a litter of kittens for a day.

Closing

ALTERNATIVE TITLES FOR CATS

Czekaj, Jef. *Cat Secrets.* New York: Balzer & Bray, 2011.

Dodd, Emma. *I Don't Want a Cool Cat!* New York: Little, Brown and Company, 2010.

Ehlert, Lois. *Boo to You!* New York: Beach Lane Books, 2009.

———. *Top Cat.* San Diego, CA: Harcourt Brace, 1998.

Fleming, Denise. *Mama Cat Has Three Kittens.* New York: Henry Holt, 1998.

Galdone, Paul. *The Three Little Kittens.* New York: Clarion Books, 1986.

Martin, Bill. *Kitty Cat, Kitty Cat, Are You Waking Up?* Tarrytown, NY: Marshall Cavendish Children, 2008.

Mockford, Caroline. *Cleo and Caspar.* New York: Barefoot Books, 2001.

Peters, Stephanie True. *Rumble Tum.* New York: Dutton Children's Books, 2009.

Schoonmaker, Elizabeth. *Square Cat.* New York: Alladin, 2011.

Volkmann, Roy. *Curious Kittens.* New York: Doubleday Book for Young Readers, 2001.

Fall, Week 3

Colors

Opening

Book 1

Mouse Paint by Ellen Stoll Walsh. San Diego, CA: Harcourt Brace Jovanovich, 1989.

- Three white mice play in jars of red, yellow and blue paint to avoid the cat.

Interactive Activity: Tiny Mouse, Tiny Mouse Magnet Board

Download pattern 2.5 at alaeditions.org/webextras.

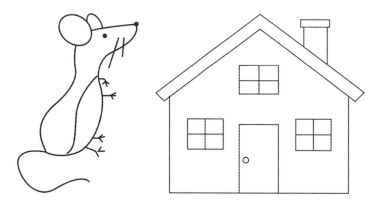

(Put the colored houses on your magnet board. Have the children cover their eyes. Put the mouse under one house. Have the children uncover their eyes and say the rhyme. Select a child to guess which house the mouse might be visiting. Peek under the house the child named and say the appropriate line. Let the children keep guessing until the mouse is found. After he's been found, have the children cover their eyes and play again and again and again. The children like playing until the mouse has visited all the colored houses.)

Tiny mouse, tiny mouse
I'm knocking on your *(color)* house.
Tiny mouse, tiny mouse
Are you in the *(color)* house?

Music & Movement

Sound recording: track 4, "If You're Wearing Colors." *Get Funky and Musical Fun with the Learning Station* by Learning Station. Melbourne, FL: Learning Station, 2003, compact disc.

- Before playing the song, have the children look and discuss what colors are on their clothes. Play the song and have the children complete the activities for clothes they are wearing.

Transition 1: Wiggle All Around

(Follow motions described, to the tune of "Jingle Bells.")
Clap your hands, stomp your feet,
Wiggle all around.
Reach your hands high in the air,
And now let's touch the ground!
Hold your hips, hold your head,
Give yourself a hug.
Sit right down, eyes to look . . .
(after look use a long pause to prepare for opening your next book)
It's time to read a book.

Book 2

Beaumont, Karen. *I Ain't Gonna Paint No More!* by Karen Beaumont. Orlando, FL: Harcourt, 2005.

- A child delights in painting the most unusual places.

Interactive Activity: Make a Rainbow Flannelboard

Download patterns 2.6 a, b, and c at alaeditions.org/webextras.

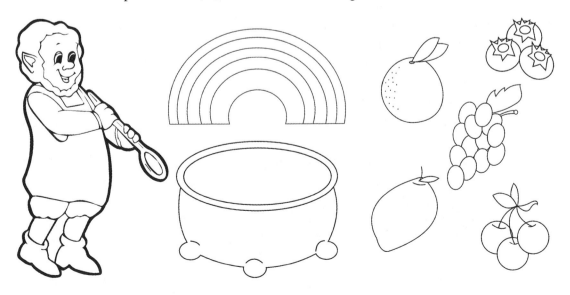

(Place the lepruchaun and pot on one side of the flannelboard. Build the rainbow on the other side.)

Take some CHERRIES, put them in a pot. *(put the cherries above the pot)*
Stir them, stir them, stir them a lot!
Pour it out now, what will it be?
The prettiest RED you ever did see. *(put red strip at top of flannelboard)*
. . . an ORANGE . . . ORANGE *(put under red strip)*
. . . a LEMON . . . YELLOW *(put under orange strip)*
. . . a LIME . . . GREEN *(put under yellow strip)*
. . . BERRIES . . . BLUE *(put under green strip)*
. . . GRAPES . . . PURPLE *(put under blue strip)*
Red and orange, yellow and green.
Blue and purple, colors are seen!
Put them together, what will it be?
The prettiest RAINBOW you ever did see.

Music & Movement

Sound recording: track 11, "Color Song." *Where Is Thumbkin?* by Learning Station. Long Branch, NJ: Kimbo Educational, 1996, compact disc.
   - Use with ribbon wands. Instruct the children to wave their ribbons when the ribbon color they are holding is being sung about. Give a safety reminder before passing out the wands. Keep sticks in their own space so as not to poke another child.

Transition 2: Hands on My Head

(Follow motions described.)
My hands upon my head I'll place.
Upon my shoulders, on my face,
At my waist, and by my side.
Then behind me they will hide.
Then I'll raise them way up high,
And let my fingers fly, fly, fly.
Then clap, clap, clap them—
1—2—3!
Sit down and see how quiet I can be. *(sit and fold hands in lap)*

Book 3

Eye Spy Colors by Debbie MacKinnon. Watertown, MA: Charlesbridge, 1998.
- Children guess familiar items by looking through a die-cut eye.

Closing

ALTERNATIVE TITLES FOR COLORS

Blackstone, Stella. *Cleo's Colors*. Cambridge, MA: Barefoot Books, 2006.

Cabrera, Jane. *Cat's Colors*. New York: Dial Books for Young Readers, 1997.

Grubb, Lisa. *Happy Dog*. New York: Philomel Books, 2003.

Hubbard, Patricia. *My Crayons Talk*. New York: Henry Holt, 1996.

McCue, Lisa. *Quiet Bunny's Many Colors*. New York: Sterling Publishing Company, 2010.

Peek, Merle. *Mary Wore Her Red Dress and Henry Wore His Green Sneakers*. New York: Clarion Books, 1985.

Sattler, Jennifer Gordon. *Sylvie*. New York: Random House, 2009.

Tafuri, Nancy. *Blue Goose*. New York: Simon & Schuster Books for Young Readers, 2008.

Tidholm, Anna-Clara. *Knock! Knock!* San Francisco, CA: Mackenzie Smiles, 2009.

ALTERNATE FLANNELBOARD ACTIVITY: "THE RAINBOW SONG"

Sound recording: track 4, "The Rainbow Song." *Barney's Greatest Hits: The Early Years*. Capitol Records, 2000, compact disc.
- Download pattern 2.7 at alaeditions.org/webextras.
- Place the pieces on the flannelboard to accompany the song lyrics.

Fall, Week 4

Farms

Opening

Book 1

Big Red Barn by Margaret Wise Brown. New York: Harper & Row, 1989.

- Rhyming text introduces the many animals that live in a barn.

Interactive Activity: Build a Scarecrow Magnet Board

Download pattern 2.8 at alaeditions.org/webextras.

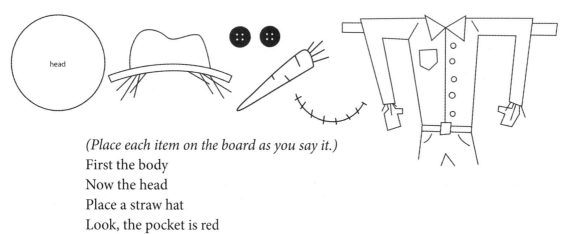

(Place each item on the board as you say it.)
First the body
Now the head
Place a straw hat
Look, the pocket is red
Some buttons for eyes
And a carrot nose
The mouth is of stitches
In two smiling rows

Music & Movement

Sound recording: track 11, "I Know a Chicken." *Whaddaya Think of That?* by Laurie Berkner. New York: Two Tomatoes, 1997, compact disc.

- Use with egg shakers. Hold shakers quiet as children repeat the echo to each line. On the last line, shake eggs.

I know a chicken, *(echo)*
And she laid an egg. *(echo)*

Oh, I know a chicken, *(echo)*
And she laid an egg. *(echo)*
Oh my goodness, (echo)
It's a shaky egg! *(echo)*
Shake your eggs!

Transition 1: Wiggle All Around

(Follow motions described, to the tune of "Jingle Bells.")
Clap your hands, stomp your feet,
Wiggle all around.
Reach your hands high in the air,
And now let's touch the ground!
Hold your hips, hold your head,
Give yourself a hug.
Sit right down, eyes to look . . .
   (after look use a long pause to prepare for opening your next book)
It's time to read a book.

Book 2

Mrs. Wishy-Washy's Farm by Joy Cowley. New York: Philomel Books, 2003.
   - Tired of being washed, a cow, a pig, and a duck leave their farm and head
   for the city.

Interactive Activity: Old MacDonald Monkey Mitt

Sing the Old MacDonald song as you place the farm animals onto your monkey mitt. Encourage the children to sing along.

Music & Movement

Sound recording: track 9, "Down on Grandpa's Farm." *One Light, One Sun*
by Raffi. Willowdale, ON: Shoreline Records, 1985, distributed by Rounder
Records (1996), compact disc.
   - Children can dance individually or swing with a partner hoedown-style.

Transition 2: Hands on My Head

(Follow motions described.)
My hands upon my head I'll place.
Upon my shoulders, on my face,
At my waist, and by my side.

(continued)

Then behind me they will hide.
Then I'll raise them way up high,
And let my fingers fly, fly, fly.
Then clap, clap, clap them—
1—2—3!
Sit down and see how quiet I can be.

Book 3

Barnyard Banter by Denise Fleming. New York: Holt, 1994.
  - All the animals are in place on the farm—except for Goose. Children cluck, muck, mew, and coo in search of Goose.

Closing

ALTERNATIVE TITLES FOR FARMS

Cimarusti, Marie Torres. *Peek-a-Moo.* NY: Dutton's Children's Books, 1998.

Hill, Eric. *Spot Goes to the Farm.* New York: Putnam, 1987.

———. *Spot's Harvest.* New York: G. P. Putnam's Sons, 2010.

Lawrence, John. *This Little Chick.* Cambridge, MA: Candlewick Press, 2002.

Most, Bernard. *Cock-a-Doodle-Moo.* San Diego, CA: Harcourt Brace, 1996.

Murphy, Mary. *How Kind.* Cambridge, MA: Candlewick Press, 2002.

Ransom, Candice F. *Tractor Day.* New York: Walker & Co., Holtzbrinck Publishers, 2007.

Tafuri, Nancy. *Spots, Feathers, and Curly Tails.* New York: Greenwillow Books, 1988.

———. *This Is the Farmer.* New York: Greenwillow Books, 1994.

Fall, Week 5

Monkeys and Jungles

Opening

Book 1

Caps for Sale: A Tale of a Peddler, Some Monkeys, and Their Monkey Business
by Esphyr Slobodkina. New York: W.R. Scott, 1947.
   - A group of monkeys steal every one of a peddler's caps while he naps
   under a tree.

Use with paper plate hats. Stack colored paper hats on your head. When the
peddler falls asleep, give each child a colored paper hat. As each monkey
throws their hat, have the children throw the plates on the floor and do as the
monkeys do.

Interactive Activity: A Picture for Mama Flannelboard

Based on the book *Bread and Honey* by Frank Asch. New York: Dutton Children's Books, 1982.
   - Download pattern 2.9 at alaeditions.org/webextras.

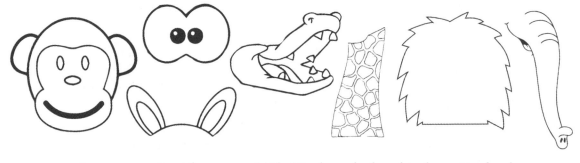

Once upon a time there was a Little Monkey who loved to draw. At school,
   his teacher asked him to draw a picture of the most beautiful thing in
   the world. Of course, his picture was of Mama Monkey. *(place face on
   flannelboard)*
He showed his picture to his friend owl. "Nice picture," said Owl. "But you
   made her eyes too small."

(continued)

"How's this?" asked Monkey. *(add larger eyes)*

"Much better," said Owl.

Next, Little Monkey showed his picture to Rabbit. "It looks just like Mama," said Rabbit, "except the ears are too small."

"How's that?" asked Little Monkey? *(add larger ears)*

"Big improvement," said Rabbit.

Crocodile was sitting close by, so Little Monkey showed the picture to her. "Pretty," said Crocodile, "But she hasn't got enough teeth."

"How's that?" asked Little Monkey? *(add large mouth with teeth)*

"Beautiful," said Crocodile.

Little Monkey liked his picture, and he couldn't wait to show his mother. On his walk home from school he talked to the crossing guard, Mrs. Giraffe. "What have you got there, Little Monkey?" Mrs. Giraffe asked. Little Monkey showed her, saying, "A picture of my mother."

"That's a lovely picture, Little Monkey, but the most beautiful mothers have long, long necks."

"Oh," said Little Monkey. "Okay!" Little Monkey got out his crayons and drew a long neck. *(place neck on monkey)*

Little Monkey continued to walk home. His neighbor, Mr. Lion was raking leaves. Mr. Lion said, "Little Monkey, I see you've got a picture there! It's looking good. But I think you forgot to add a full mane of hair."

"Yes, okay," Little Monkey said. He got out his crayons, added the mane, and crossed the street. *(add mane)*

Little Monkey was almost home. Sitting out on her sunporch was his nosy neighbor, Ms. Elephant. Ms. Elephant wanted to hear all about Little Monkey's day.

"I'm glad to see you, Ms. Elephant," Little Monkey said. "But I really can't wait to get home to my mother. I've got—"

"Whoa! What's that?" Ms. Elephant asked.

"It's a picture of my mother," Little Monkey said.

"Well, it's really quite good," Ms. Elephant said. "It's got lots of colors and you stayed in your lines. The only trouble is . . ."

"What?" said Little Monkey.

"Your mother would certainly look more beautiful with a longer nose."

"Okay," Little Monkey said. He got out his crayons and drew a long nose. *(place trunk on board)*

Finally, Little Monkey was home. Inside, Mama Monkey was fixing Little Monkey's snack. "Hello, Little Monkey!" she said.

"I made a picture for you at school today. It is a picture of the most beautiful thing in the world." Little Monkey said. He gave his mother the picture.

"Why, that IS beautiful, Little Monkey," Mama Monkey said. "Who is it?"

"It's *you*, Mom!" Little Monkey said.

Mama Monkey took the picture and hung it up on the middle of the refrigerator. Then, she gave Little Monkey a BIG monkey hug.

"Thank you, Little Monkey, I love it!"

Music & Movement

Sound recording: track 2, "No More Monkeys." *Animal Playground: Playful Tracks from Around the World*. New York: Putumayo World Music, 2007, compact disc.

(Challenge the children to jump throughout the song. If they need a rest, they can stop and pretend to make a phone call to the doctor.)

Now five monkeys were playing on the bed.

One fell off and bumped his head.

So Mommy called the doctor and the doctor said,

"No more monkeys jumping on the bed!"

That is what the doctor said.

Four little monkeys . . .

Three little monkeys . . .

Two little monkeys . . .

Now one monkey was playing on his bed

He fell off and bumped his head.

Mommy called the children and the children said,

"Yes, more monkeys jumping on the bed!"

That is what the doctor said.

Transition 1: Wiggle All Around

(Follow motions described, to the tune of "Jingle Bells.")

Clap your hands, stomp your feet,

Wiggle all around.

Reach your hands high in the air,

And now let's touch the ground!

Hold your hips, hold your head,

Give yourself a hug.

Sit right down, eyes to look . . .

   (after look *use a long pause to prepare for opening your next book)*

It's time to read a book.

Book 2

Starry Safari by Linda Ashman. Orlando, FL: Harcourt, 2005.

- A young girl's imagination takes her on an African safari.

Interactive Activity: Five Little Monkeys Monkey Mitt

(Use with crocodile puppet and five monkeys on the monkey mitt. Quietly say, "Along came Mr. Alligator," and then SNAP loudly. Have the alligator snap a monkey off the mitt. After all monkeys are in the alligator's mouth and he has swum away, show the children that the monkeys are still there and everyone is okay.)

Five little monkeys swinging in the tree.
Teasing Mr. Alligator: "Can't catch me. . . . can't catch me!"
Along came Mr. Alligator, quiet as can be,
And snapped that monkey out of that tree!

Four little monkeys . . .
Three little monkeys . . .
Two little monkeys . . .
One little monkey . . .

No more monkeys swinging in the tree.
Away swims Mr. Alligator—
He's fat as fat can be.

Music & Movement

Sound recording: track 9, "Monkey Talk." *Little Ditties for Itty Bitties* by Michele Valeri. New York: Community Music, 2010, compact disc.

- Children can dance and scratch their underarms during "Oooh-ooo-aa-aahs." Then do the actions of the monkeys as they search for bananas.

Transition 2: Hands on My Head

(Follow motions described.)
My hands upon my head I'll place.
Upon my shoulders, on my face,
At my waist, and by my side.
Then behind me they will hide.
Then I'll raise them way up high,
And let my fingers fly, fly, fly.
Then clap, clap, clap them—
1—2—3!
Sit down and see how quiet I can be. *(sit and fold hands in lap)*

Book 3

Hug by Jez Alborough. Cambridge, MA: Candlewick Press, 2000.
   - Bobo the chimp seeks hugs among various jungle animals and their babies.

Closing

ALTERNATIVE TITLES FOR MONKEYS AND JUNGLES

Browne, Anthony. *Willy the Dreamer*. Cambridge, MA: Candlewick Press, 1998.

Butler, John. *Whose Nose and Toes?* New York: Viking, 2004.

Christelow, Eileen. *Five Little Monkeys Jumping on the Bed*. New York: Clarion Books, 1989.

MacLennon, Cathy. *Monkey Monkey Monkey*. London: Boxer, 2009.

Mallat, Kathy. *Mama Love*. New York: Walker & Co, 2004.

Patricelli, Leslie. *Be Quiet, Mike!* Somerville, MA: Candlewick Press, 2011.

Slack, Michael. *Monkey Truck*. New York: Henry Holt, 2011.

Taylor, Thomas. *The Loudest Roar*. New York: Arthur A. Levine Books, 2002.

Tierney, Fiona. *Lion's Lunch?* New York: Chicken House, 2010.

Fall, Week 6

Sweets

Opening

Book 1

Sitting Down to Eat by Bill Harley. Little Rock, AR: August House Little Folk, 1996.

    - A young boy agrees to share his snack with a growing group of uninvited animal guests.

Interactive Activity: What a Cake Magnet Board

Download patterns 2.10 a and b at alaeditions.org/webextras.

Once there was a baker who baked a lovely cake. *(put cake on board)*
Oh, what a cake he did make!
But when he wasn't looking,
A flea flew in *(add flea)*
To the cake the baker baked.
Oh, what a cake THAT did make.

But when he wasn't looking,
A butterfly blew in *(add butterfly)*

To where the flea flew
In the cake the baker baked.
Oh, what a cake THAT did make.

But when he wasn't looking,
A frog flipped in *(add frog)*
To where the butterfly blew
And the flea flew
In the cake the baker baked.
Oh, what a cake THAT did make.

But when he wasn't looking,
A mouse marched in *(add mouse)*
To where the frog flipped
And the butterfly blew
And the flea flew
In the cake the baker baked.
Oh, what a cake THAT did make.

But when he wasn't looking,
A duck danced in *(add duck)*
To where the mouse marched
And the frog flipped
And the butterfly blew
And the flea flew
In the cake the baker baked.
Oh, what a cake THAT did make.

But when he wasn't looking,
A pig pranced in *(add pig)*
To where the duck danced
And the mouse marched
And the frog flipped
And the butterfly blew
And the flea flew
In the cake the baker baked.
Oh, what a cake THAT did make.

But then the baker looked and said, "Enough!"
(remove each animal as you say their name)
And out the pig pranced,
And out the duck danced,
And out the mouse marched,
And out the frog flipped,

(continued)

And out the butterfly blew,
And out the flea flew.
And they all SHARED the cake the baker baked.
And what a cake he did make!

Music & Movement

Sound recording: track 2, "Sticky Bubble Gum." *Sticky Bubble Gum and Other Tasty Tunes: Sing Along, Dance Along, Do Along* by Carole Peterson. United States: Macaroni Soup, 2002, compact disc.

(Clap hands together from side to side and follow the motions described. On un-stick pull hands off and start clapping for the next verse.)

Sticky, sticky, sticky bubblegum,
Bubblegum, bubblegum.
Sticky, sticky, sticky bubblegum,
Sticking your hands to your shoes . . . UN-STICK!
. . . your knees to your elbows . . .
. . . your toe to your nose . . .
. . . your hand to someone else's hand . . .
. . . your back to someone else's back . . .
. . . your head to the floor . . .

Transition 1: Wiggle All Around

(Follow motions described, to the tune of "Jingle Bells.")
Clap your hands, stomp your feet,
Wiggle all around.
Reach your hands high in the air,
And now let's touch the ground!
Hold your hips, hold your head,
Give yourself a hug.
Sit right down, eyes to look . . .
    (after look *use a long pause to prepare for opening your next book)*
It's time to read a book.

Book 2

Bubble Gum, Bubble Gum by Lisa Wheeler. New York: Little, Brown and Co, 2004.

- A variety of animals get stuck in bubblegum melting in the road. They must survive encounters with a truck and a bear.

Interactive Activity: Ice Cream Super Scoopers Flannelboard

Download pattern 2.11 at alaeditions.org/webextras.

Once there was a little boy who loved ice cream.

Do any of YOU like ice cream?

(pause to allow the children to yell out their favorite flavors)

Good.

This little boy liked the same kinds of ice cream you do.

He liked chocolate. And he liked vanilla and grape and orange and chocolate ripple . . . *(add the flavors the children have suggested)*

One day his mother gave him money to buy an ice cream cone.

"Oh! Wow," thought the little boy. I can get any kind I want. And right away he picked strawberry. *(add cone and pink scoop to flannelboard)*

That looked so good he took a big lick!

Slurp!

But then he looked again and he saw the *(other flavor)* ice cream.

And he decided to have that too.

The strawberry-*(other flavor)* cone looked so good he took a big lick.

Slurp!

(continue adding until all the flavors are piled on the cone)

Now the boy was happy!

He had a strawberry, vanilla, mint chocolate chip, lime, cherry, blueberry, orange, chocolate chip, lemon, and grape ice cream cone.

And he took a big lick of the strawberry.

(continued)

Slurp! *(Remove pink and continue licking and removing one scoop at a time until all the flavors are gone. Ask children to recall the flavors as you remove them.)*
And then he ate the cone and said,
"Yum, yum! That was just the kind of ice cream I wanted." *(remove cone)*

Music & Movement

Sound recording: track 18: "Milkshake." *Songs for Wiggleworms.* Chicago, IL: Old Town School of Folk Music, 2000, compact disc.
    - Follow the lyrics by pretending to pour, stir, and so on. On *shake*, the children should jump as fast as possible.

Transition 2: Hands on My Head

(Follow motions described.)
My hands upon my head I'll place.
Upon my shoulders, on my face,
At my waist, and by my side.
Then behind me they will hide.
Then I'll raise them way up high,
And let my fingers fly, fly, fly.
Then clap, clap, clap them—
1—2—3!
Sit down and see how quiet I can be. *(sit and fold hands in lap)*

Book 3

If You Give a Mouse a Cookie by Laura Joffe Numeroff. New York: Harper & Row, 1985.
    - The consequences of giving a cookie to a mouse run the reader ragged.

Closing

ALTERNATIVE TITLES FOR SWEETS

Hayward, Linda. *Baker, Baker, Cookie Maker.* New York: Random House, 1998.

Meadows, Michelle. *Piggies in the Kitchen.* New York: Simon & Schuster Books for Young Readers, 2011.

Moffatt, Judith. *Who Stole the Cookies?* New York: Grosset & Dunlap, 1996.

Numeroff, Laura Joffe. *If You Give a Cat a Cupcake.* New York: Laura Geringer Books, 2008.

Staake, Bob. *The Donut Chef.* New York: Golden Books, 2008.

Wellington, Monica. *Mr. Cookie Baker.* New York: Dutton Children's Books, 2006.

Wilson, Karma. *The Cow Loves Cookies.* New York: Margaret K. McElderry Books, 2010.

Winter, Week 1

Birthdays and Months of the Year

Opening

Book 1

All the Seasons of the Year by Deborah Lee Rose. New York: Abrams Books for Young Readers, 2010.

- Mother Cat loves little kitty throughout all the seasons of the year.

Interactive Activity: Five Little Candles Flannelboard

Download pattern 2.12 at alaeditions.org/webextras.

(Encourage the children to join you as you exaggerate the blowing out of each candle.)

Five candles on a birthday cake.

Just five and not one more.

(continued)

You may blow out one—
And that leaves four.

Four candles on a birthday cake
For all to see.
You may blow out one—
And that leaves three.

Three candles on a birthday cake
Standing straight and blue.
You may blow out another one—
And that leaves two.

Two candles on a birthday cake.
Birthdays are great fun.
You may blow one candle out—
And that leaves one.

One candle on a birthday cake.
We know our work is done.
You may blow the last candle out—
And that leaves none.

Music & Movement

Sound recording: track 2, "Birthday Bee Bop." *Birthday Party Songs* by Kim Mitzo Thompson. New York: Twin Sisters, 2001, compact disc.

- In hokey-pokey fashion, follow the caller's instructions. On the chorus, clap and jump.

Transition 1: Johnny Thumbs Up

(Follow motions described.)
Johnny thumbs up, Johnny thumbs down.
Johnny thumbs dancing all around the town.
Dance them on your shoulders,
Dance them on your head.
Dance them on your knees,
Then tuck them into bed. *(fold hands and sit down)*

Book 2

Birthday Zoo by Deborah Lee Rose. Morton Grove, IL: A. Whitman, 2002.
    - The animals of the zoo prepare a birthday party.

Interactive Activity: When This Bag Is Full Prop Activity

Based on the book *When This Box Is Full* by Patricia Lille. New York: Greenwillow Books, 1993.

> This bag is empty . . . but not for long.
> I will fill it . . .
> In JANUARY with a MITTEN.
> In FEBRUARY with a CANDY HEART.
> In MARCH with a SHAMROCK.
> In APRIL with a purple plastic EASTER EGG.
> In MAY with a TULIP.
> In JUNE with a SAND SHOVEL.
> In JULY with an AMERICAN FLAG.
> In AUGUST with an ICE CREAM CONE.
> In SEPTEMBER with a RED APPLE.
> In OCTOBER with an ORANGE LEAF.
> In NOVEMBER with a WISHBONE from a turkey.
> In DECEMBER with a TREE ORNAMENT.
> And then, I'll share the bag with you!

Music & Movement

Sound recording: track 9, "Simon Says." *Birthday Party Songs* by Kim Mitzo Thompson. New York: Twin Sisters, 2001, compact disc.
    - Follow the recording to play the classic birthday game.

Transition 2: I Can Wiggle

> *(Wiggle each body part.)*
> I can wiggle my fingers,
> I can wiggle my toes.
> I can wiggle my shoulders,
> And I can wiggle my nose.
> I can wiggle the wiggles
> All out of me. *(wiggle whole body robustly)*
> And I can sit
> As still as can be. *(sit down and fold hands)*

Book 3

When Lucy Goes Out Walking by Ashley Wolff. New York: Christy Ottaviano Books, 2009.

- The puppy Lucy enjoys walking through all the seasons of the year. As the seasons change, Lucy grows up.

Closing

ALTERNATIVE TITLES FOR BIRTHDAYS AND MONTHS OF THE YEAR

Bauer, Marion Dane. *In Like a Lion, Out Like a Lamb.* New York: Holiday House, 2011.

Bunting, Eve. *Sing a Song of Piglets: A Calendar in Verse.* New York: Clarion Books, 2002.

Christelow, Eileen. *Five Little Monkeys Bake a Birthday Cake* (formerly titled *Don't Wake Up Mama*). Five Little Monkeys Picture Books series. New York: Clarion Books, 1992.

Hayles, Marsha. *Pajamas Anytime.* New York: G. P. Putnam's Sons, 2005.

Lord, Cynthia. *Happy Birthday, Hamster.* New York: Scholastic Press, 2011.

Na, Il Sung. *Snow Rabbit, Spring Rabbit: A Book of Changing Seasons.* New York: Alfred A Knopf, 2010.

Robart, Rose. *The Cake That Mack Ate.* Boston, MA: Atlantic Monthly Press, 1986.

Schoenherr, Ian. *Don't Spill the Beans.* New York: Greenwillow Books, 2010.

Sperring, Mark. *The Fairytale Cake.* New York: Scholastic, 2005.

Thomas, Jan. *A Birthday for Cow.* Orlando, FL: Harcourt, 2008.

Yolen, Jane. *How Do Dinosaurs Say Happy Birthday?* New York: The Blue Sky Press, 2011.

Winter, Week 2

Colds & Sneezes

Opening

Book 1

Tissue, Please! by Lisa Kopelke. New York: Simon & Schuster Books for Young Readers, 2004.

- Frog's parents show frog and his friends that it is better to use a tissue when your nose is stuffy.

Music & Movement

Sound recording: track 8, "A-Goong Went the Little Green Frog." *Favorite Sing-a-Longs Volumes 1–3.* St. Laurent, Quebec, Canada: Madacy Entertainment Group, 2000, compact disc.

- Use with scarves or tissues. Substitute "achoo" for "a-goong" and pretend to sneeze into scarf.

Interactive Activity: Five Pretty Flowers Flannelboard

Download pattern 2.13 at alaeditions.org/webextras.

(Encourage children to join you when you sneeze playfully and with exaggeration.)
Five pretty flowers
In the meadow grew.
"Hmmmm," I said.
"I bet they smell pretty too!"
I bent down to sniff,
But they tickled my nose!
Ah-chooo! Oh no!
Away one flower blows!

Four pretty flowers . . .
Three pretty flowers . . .
Two pretty flowers . . .
One pretty flower . . .

Transition 1: Johnny Thumbs Up

(Follow motions described.)
Johnny thumbs up, Johnny thumbs down.
Johnny thumbs dancing all around the town.
Dance them on your shoulders,
Dance them on your head.
Dance them on your knees,
Then tuck them into bed. *(fold hands and sit down)*

Book 2

Barn Sneeze by Karen B. Honesdale. PA: Boyds Mills Press, 2002.
  - Sue's farm animals all have a case of the sneezes.

Interactive Activity: Five Hungry Ants Flannelboard

Download pattern 2.14 at alaeditions.org/webextras.

*(Before sneezing, pretend to sprinkle a little of the pepper on
    each ant. Remove one ant as you sneeze.)*
Five hungry ants,
Marching in a line.
Came upon a picnic
Where they could dine.
They marched into the salad,
They marched into the cake,
They marched into the pepper,
Uh-oh! That was a mistake!
Achoooo!

Four hungry ants . . .
Three hungry ants . . .
Two hungry ants . . .
One hungry ant . . .

Music & Movement

Sound recording: track 3, "Clap, Clap, Clap Your Hands." *Sticky Bubble Gum and Other Tasty Tunes: Sing Along, Dance Along, Do Along* by Carole Peterson. United States: Macaroni Soup, 2002, compact disc.

- Clap, stamp, and jump as directed. On the la-la-la-las, slowly turn around in circles.

Transition 2: I Can Wiggle

(Wiggle each body part.)
I can wiggle my fingers,
I can wiggle my toes.
I can wiggle my shoulders,
And I can wiggle my nose.
I can wiggle the wiggles
All out of me. *(wiggle whole body robustly)*
And I can sit
As still as can be. *(sit down and fold hands)*

Book 3

The Flea's Sneeze by Lynn Downey. New York: Holt, 2000.

- A flea in the barn startles all the animals when he sneezes.

Closing

ALTERNATIVE TITLES FOR COLDS AND SNEEZES

Redmond, E. S. *Felicity Floo Visits the Zoo*. New York: Candlewick Press, 2009.

Thomas, Patricia. *"Stand Back," Said the Elephant, "I'm Going to Sneeze!"* New York: Lothrop, Lee & Shepard Books, 1990.

Willems, Mo. *Pigs Make Me Sneeze! An Elephant & Piggie Book*. New York: Hyperion Books for Children, 2009.

Wright, Maureen. *Sneeze, Big Bear, Sneeze!* Tarrytown, NY: Marshall Cavendish Children, 2011.

———. *Sneezy the Snowman*. Tarrytown, NY: Marshall Cavendish Children, 2010.

Winter, Week 3

Dogs

Opening

Book 1

Feiffer, Jules. *Bark, George.* New York: HarperCollins, 1999.
- George's mother takes him to the vet when he has lost his ability to bark.

Interactive Activity: Harley's Colorful Day Flannelboard Story

- Based on the book *Dog's Colorful Day: A Messy Story about Colors and Counting* by Emma Dodd. New York: Dutton Children's Books, 2000.
- Download pattern 2.15 at alaeditions.org/webextras.

(As you read each color, place the circle of corresponding flannel on Harley. After his bath, place Harley without the colored spots on the rug. As you count the ten spots, encourage the children to count with you. When you review the stain sources, see how many the children can recall.)

This is Harley.
As you can see, Harley is white with one black spot on his left ear.
At breakfast time, Harley sits under the table.
Splash! A drip of ORANGE juice lands on his back.
Now Harley has two spots.
After breakfast he runs outside.
He slips past the man painting the fence.
Splat! His ear hits the GRAY paint.
Now Harley has three spots.

Harley rolls on the grass to get off that paint.

Smudge! The grass makes a GREEN stain on his white fur.

Now Harley has four spots.

Harley takes his walk to the park.

His owner is eating chocolate ice cream.

Dribble! The ice creams drips onto Harley, and he has a BROWN spot.

Now Harley has five spots.

A bumblebee wants to taste that ice cream.

Swish! The bee drops YELLOW pollen on Harley as it has a lick.

Now Harley has six spots.

Harley trots on through the park.

Stick! A glob of PINK bubblegum smells delicious to Harley.

It sticks near his nose, and now Harley has seven spots.

Harley turns back and begins his trip home.

Splash! A bouncing ball splatters Harley with water from a BLUE puddle.

Now Harley has eight spots.

In front of his yard, Harley's little girl is playing hopscotch, and Harley
     steps on her RED sidewalk chalk.

Smear! A patch of RED appears on his leg.

Now Harley has nine spots.

Harley races back inside the house and knocks right into Mom.

"Silly Harley!" Mom's pen leaves a PURPLE smudge on Harley's head.

Now Harley has ten spots.

Mom looks down at Harley.

She counts his colorful spots.

1–2–3–4–5–6–7–8–9–10!

An ORANGE splash of juice.

A GRAY smear of paint.

A GREEN patch from grass.

A BROWN drop of ice cream.

A YELLOW patch of pollen.

A PINK glob of bubblegum.

A BLUE splatter from a puddle.

A RED spot of sidewalk chalk.

A PURPLE smudge of ink.

And, of course, a black spot on Harley's ear.

"You need a bath, Harley," Mom decides.

When Harley snuggles next to his family on his RUG, he has just one spot
     on his left ear.

"Sweet dreams, Harley. What a colorful day you've had!"

Music & Movement

Sound recording: track 4, "Do Your Ears Hang Low?" *Kids Nursery Rhymes.*
Volume 1. United States: MasterSong, 2001, compact disc.

Do your ears hang low?
Do they wobble to and fro? *(use hands to mimic long, waving ears)*
Can you tie them in a knot?
Can you tie them in a bow? *(pretend to tie bow on top of head)*
Can you throw them o'er your shoulder
Like a continental soldier? *(salute and stand at attention)*
Do your ears hang low?

Do your ears hang high?
Do they reach up to the sky? *(jump up high)*
Do they wrinkle when they're wet?
Do they straighten when they're dry? *(pretend to straighten ears)*
Can you wave them at your neighbor
With an element of flavor? *(wave ears to each other)*
Do your ears hang high?

Do your ears hang wide?
Do they flap from side to side? *(wiggle hands outward from ears)*
Do they wave in the breeze
From the slightest little sneeze? *(pretend to sneeze)*
Can you soar above the nation
With a feeling of elevation? *(jump up high)*
Do your ears hang wide?

Transition 1: Johnny Thumbs Up

(Follow motions described.)
Johnny thumbs up, Johnny thumbs down.
Johnny thumbs dancing all around the town.
Dance them on your shoulders,
Dance them on your head.
Dance them on your knees,
Then tuck them into bed. *(fold hands and sit down)*

Book 2

Where's Pup? by Dayle Ann Dodds. New York: Dial Books for Young Readers,
2003.

- A circus clown's search for his partner leads him all the way to the top of
a pyramid of acrobats.

Interactive Activity: BINGO Flannelboard

Download pattern 2.16 at alaeditions.org/webextras. As you sing the song, remove the circle with the letter on it when it is dropped from the lyrics. Clap as the letters disappear.

There was a farmer had a dog and Bingo was his name-o.
B-I-N-G-O
B-I-N-G-O
B-I-N-G-O and Bingo was his name-o.

(clap)-I-N-G-O
(clap)-*(clap)*-N-G-O
(clap)-*(clap)*-*(clap)*-G-O
(clap)-*(clap)*-*(clap)*-*(clap)*-O
(clap)-*(clap)*-*(clap)*-*(clap)*-*(clap)*

Music & Movement

Sound recording: track 5, "Wiggy Wiggles Freeze Dance." *Two Little Sounds: Fun with Phonics and Numbers* by Hap Palmer. Topanga, CA: Hap-Pal Music, 2003, compact disc.

- Instruct the children to dance when the music is playing but to listen carefully and freeze when the music stops. It is fun to use egg shakers or rhythm instruments with this activity too.

Transition 2: I Can Wiggle

(Wiggle each body part.)
I can wiggle my fingers,
I can wiggle my toes.
I can wiggle my shoulders,
And I can wiggle my nose.
I can wiggle the wiggles
All out of me. (wiggle whole body robustly)
And I can sit
As still as can be. *(sit down and fold hands)*

Book 3

Ten Puppies by Lynn Reiser. New York: Greenwillow Books, 2003.
   - Ten puppies are counted and sorted by their different features.

Closing

ALTERNATIVE TITLES FOR DOGS

Dodd, Emma. *I Don't Want a Posh Dog!* New York: Little, Brown, 2008.

Ehlert, Lois. *Rrralph.* New York: Beach Lane Books, 2011.

Flather, Lisa. *Ten Silly Dogs: A Countdown Story.* New York: Orchard Books, 1999.

George, Lindsey Barrett. *That Pup!* New York: Greenwillow Books, 2011.

Graham, Bob. *"Let's Get a Pup!" Said Kate.* Cambridge, MA: Candlewick Press, 2001.

Hubbell, Patricia. *Shaggy Dogs, Waggy Dogs.* Tarrytown, NY: Marshall Cavendish Children, 2011.

Joosse, Barbara. *Dog Parade.* New York: Houghton Mifflin Harcourt Publishing Co, 2011.

McDonnell, Patrick. *Wag.* New York: Little, Brown & Company for Young Readers, 2009.

Rylant, Cynthia *The Great Gracie Chase: Stop That Dog!* New York: Blue Sky Press, 2001.

Shields, Gillian. *Dogfish.* New York: Atheneum Books for Young Readers, 2008.

Winter, Week 4

Snow & Snowmen

Opening

Book 1

Frozen Noses by Jan Carr. New York: Holiday House, 1999.
  - Winter activities such as throwing snowballs, making a snowman, and ice skating are described.

Interactive Activity: The Snowman Tell and Draw Story

Tell and Draw Story: The Snowman *Tell and Draw Stories* by Margaret J. Olson. Minneapolis, MN: Creative Storytime Press, 1986.
  - Download drawing instructions 2.17 a, b, and c at alaeditions.org/webextras.

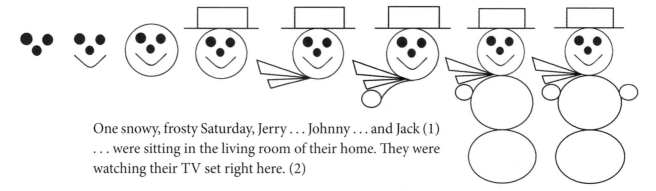

One snowy, frosty Saturday, Jerry . . . Johnny . . . and Jack (1) . . . were sitting in the living room of their home. They were watching their TV set right here. (2)

But Johnny and Jerry were tired of watching TV. They wanted to go ice skating. Jack stayed home as his favorite TV show was just coming on. But he called after them, "I'll have a surprise for you when you get back."

Johnny and Jerry went out the door and around the house like this. (3)

They were going to get their skates out of the garage. Here is the garage. (4)

It didn't take the boys long to find their skates. Johnny and Jerry had to walk up and down several streets like this (5) to get to the ice skating rink.

At the skating rink they went to the warming house right here (6) to put their skates on. W-h-e-e.

And away they went. Round and round the ice rink like this. (7) What fun they had! W-h-e-e.

They stopped in the warming house on the other side of the ice rink right here.(8) They took their skates off and started home.

When they got home the first thing they saw was Jack's surprise. Can you guess what it was? *(have children guess)*

Yes, he had built a SNOWMAN!

Music & Movement

Sound recording: track 15, "Snow Fun." *Preschool Action Time: Activities and Finger Plays* by Carole Hammett. Long Branch, NJ: Kimbo Educational, 1988, compact disc.

- Pretend to ice skate, throw snow balls, climb the slopes, and so on. When the snow is falling, make fingers flutter toward the ground like falling snowflakes.

Transition 1: Johnny Thumbs Up

(Follow motions described.)
Johnny thumbs up, Johnny thumbs down.
Johnny thumbs dancing all around the town.
Dance them on your shoulders,
Dance them on your head.
Dance them on your knees,
Then tuck them into bed. *(fold hands and sit down)*

Book 2

Mouse's First Snow by Lauren Thompson. New York: Simon & Schuster Books for Young Readers, 2005.

- Mouse tries many new activities when he goes outside to play in the snow.

Interactive Activity: Five Little Snowmen Flannelboard

Download pattern 2.18 at alaeditions.org/webextras.

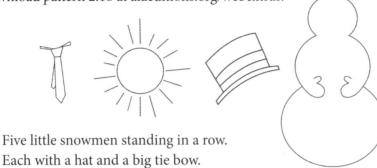

Five little snowmen standing in a row.
Each with a hat and a big tie bow.
Out came the sun, and it shined all day.
And one little snowmen melted away.

Four little snowmen . . .
Three little snowmen . . .
Two little snowmen . . .
One little snowman . . .

Music & Movement

Sound Recording: track 25, "Snowflake, Snowflake." *H.U.M. All Year Long: Highly Usable Music Kids Can Sing, Dance & Do* by Carole Peterson. United States: Macaroni Soup, 2003, compact disc.

- Use snowflake wands. The children can dance their wands in the air and make them fall to the ground as instructed in the song lyrics. They can lightly touch the body parts with their snowflakes as the lyrics indicate.

Snowflake, snowflake dance around,
Snowflake, snowflake touch the ground.
Snowflake landing on my nose,
Snowflake landing on my toes.

(continued)

Snowflake, snowflake dance around,
Snowflake, snowflake touch the ground.

Transition 2: I Can Wiggle

(Wiggle each body part.)
I can wiggle my fingers,
I can wiggle my toes.
I can wiggle my shoulders,
And I can wiggle my nose.
I can wiggle the wiggles
All out of me. *(wiggle whole body robustly)*
And I can sit
As still as can be. *(sit down and fold hands)*

Book 3

Snowballs by Lois Ehlert. San Diego, CA: Harcourt Brace, 1995.
   - Children create a family out of snow.

Closing

ALTERNATIVE TITLES FOR SNOW AND SNOWMEN

Fallon, Jimmy. *Snowball Fight.* New York: Dutton Children's Books, 2005.

Gershator, Phillis. *When It Starts to Snow.* New York: Henry Holt, 1998.

Harper, Lee. *Snow, Snow, Snow.* New York: Simon & Schuster Books for Young Readers, 2009.

Helquist, Brett. *Bedtime for Bear.* New York: Harper, 2011.

Henkes, Kevin. *Oh!* New York: Greenwillow Books, 1999.

Hoban, Julia. *Amy Loves the Snow.* New York: Harper & Row, 1989.

Hubbell, Patricia. *Snow Happy.* New York: Tricycle Press, 2010.

Joosse, Barbara M. *Snow Day.* New York: Clarion Books, 1995.

Keats, Ezra Jack. *The Snowy Day.* New York, Viking Press, 1962.

Korda, Lerryn. *Millions of Snow.* Somerville, MA: Candlewick Press, 2007.

McGhee, Alison. *Making a Friend.* New York: Atheneum Books for Young Readers, 2011.

Moser, Lisa. *Perfect Soup.* New York: Random House, 2010.

Rockwell, Anne F. *The First Snowfall.* New York: Macmillan Publishing, 1987.

Schertle, Alice. *All You Need for a Snowman.* San Diego, CA: Harcourt, 2002.

Schoenherr, Ian. *Pip and Squeak.* New York: Greenwillow Books, 2007.

Siddals, Mary McKenna. *Millions of Snowflakes.* New York: Clarion Books, 1998.

Winget, Susan. *Sam the Snowman.* New York: Harper Collins Children's Books, 2008.

Wright, Maureen. *Sneezy the Snowman.* Tarrytown, NY: Marshall Cavendish Children, 2010.

Ziefert, Harriet. *Snow Party.* Maplewood, NJ: Blue Apple Books, 2008.

Winter, Week 5

Valentine's Day and Love

Opening

Book 1

Sweet Hearts by Jan Carr. New York: Holiday House, 2002.
   - A girl hides paper hearts around her house on Valentine's Day.

Interactive Activity: Colorful Hearts Participation Rhyme

Download pattern 2.19 at alaeditions.org/webextras.

(Pass out different colored heart shapes.
   Continue repeating the rhyme until all hearts
   have been collected.)
Colored hearts, colored hearts.
Look at yours and see.
If you have a *(color)* heart,
Please bring it to me.

Music & Movement

Sound recording: track 1, "If You're Happy and You Know It." *If You're Happy and You Know It . . . : Sing Along with Bob #1* by Bob McGrath. Teaneck, NJ: Bob's Kids Music, 2000, compact disc.

- Clap, stamp, shout, and hug as directed. On "your face will surely show it," use fingers to draw a smile on your face. For older groups you can invite them to create some verses of their own when the recording is over.

Transition 1: Johnny Thumbs Up

(Follow motions described.)
Johnny thumbs up, Johnny thumbs down.
Johnny thumbs dancing all around the town.
Dance them on your shoulders,
Dance them on your head.
Dance them on your knees,
Then tuck them into bed. *(fold hands and sit down)*

Book 2

Counting Kisses by Karen Katz. New York: Margaret K. McElderry Books, 2001.

- The number of kisses a baby needs to go to sleep are counted.

Interactive Activity: Color Valentines Magnet Board

(Place one of each colored heart on magnet board as you recite rhyme.)
Valentines are pink,
Valentines can be blue.
Valentines made of red
Say, "I love you."
A valentine of purple,
A valentine of green.
By far, YOU'RE *(point to children)* the loveliest valentine
I've ever seen.

Music & Movement

Sound recording: track 30, "Skinnamarink." *If You're Happy and You Know It
. . . : Sing Along with Bob #1* by Bob McGrath. Teaneck, NJ: Bob's Kids Music,
2000, compact disc.

*(Put one hand under the opposite elbow and wave, alternating right and left
arms.)*
Skinnamarink a-dink a-dink,
Skinnamarink a-do, I love you.
Skinnamarink a-dink a-dink,
Skinnamarink a-do, I love you. *(sign I love you: point to yourself, cross fists
over heart, point to baby, and repeat with reverse hand)*
I love you in the morning, and in the afternoon, *(for morning, make low
circle using arms; for afternoon, move arms in front of body)*
I love you in the evening, underneath the moon. *(for evening, move arms
over head)*
Skinnamarink a-dink a-dink,
Skinnamarink a-do, I love you.

Transition 2: I Can Wiggle

(Wiggle each body part.)
I can wiggle my fingers,
I can wiggle my toes.
I can wiggle my shoulders,
And I can wiggle my nose.
I can wiggle the wiggles
All out of me. *(wiggle whole body robustly)*
And I can sit
As still as can be. *(sit down and fold hands)*

Book 3

Marzollo, Jean. *I Love You (A Rebus Poem)*. New York: Scholastic, 2000.
- In rebus poem format, the speaker professes love equal to that of a bird
for a tree, a flower for a bee, and a lock for a key.

Closing

ALTERNATIVE TITLES FOR VALENTINE'S DAY AND LOVE

Cocca-Leffler, Maryanne. *One Heart: A Valentine Counting Book*. New York: Cartwheel Books, 2009.

Loesser, Frank. *I Love You! A Bushel & a Peck*. New York: HarperCollins, 2005.

McGuirk, Leslie. *Tucker's Valentine*. Somerville, MA: Candlewick Press, 2010.

Rusackas, Francesca. *I Love You All Day Long*. New York: HarperCollins, 2003.

Weeks, Sarah. *Be Mine, Be Mine, Sweet Valentine*. New York: Laura Geringer Books, 2006.

Winter, Week 6

Clothes: Hats and Mittens

Opening

Book 1

The First Day of Winter by Denise Fleming. New York: Henry Holt and Company, 2005.

- A snowman comes alive as a child adds pieces to it for the first ten days of winter.

Interactive Activity: Bear Gets Dressed Flannelboard

Download patterns 2.20 a and b at alaeditions.org/webextras.

(As you dress the bear, place the clothes on the wrong body parts and encourage the children to correct you. Take each item off after its paragraph and dress the bear correctly in the last verse. Smile and act surprised as the clothing is placed correctly.)

Bear can get dressed all by himself.
This is his COAT.
Should he put it on like this? *(put on like pants)*
No!
Bear, your coat goes on your back.

These are Bear's PANTS.
Should he put them on like this? *(put on like shirt)*
No!
Bear, put your legs through the pants.

This is Bear's HAT.
Should he put it on like this? *(put on like socks)*
No!
Bear, your hat goes on your head.

These are Bear's BOOTS.
Should he put them on like this? *(put on over ears)*
No!
Boots go on feet, Bear.

Here goes . . .
Coat!
Pants!
Hat!
Boots!
Bear's ready.
Off he goes!
Bear got dressed all by himself.

Music & Movement

Sound recording: track 4, "Getting Dressed." *Music Time* by Johnette Downing. New Orleans, LA: Wiggle Worm Records, 2005, compact disc.

- Pretend to be getting dressed to accompany the lyrics.

Transition 1: Johnny Thumbs Up

(Follow motions described.)
Johnny thumbs up, Johnny thumbs down.
Johnny thumbs dancing all around the town.
Dance them on your shoulders,
Dance them on your head.
Dance them on your knees,
Then tuck them into bed. *(fold hands and sit down)*

Book 2

A Hat for Minerva Louise by Janet Morgan Stoeke. New York: Dutton Children's Books, 1994.

- A chicken uses a pair of mittens as a hat for her head and her bottom.

Interactive Activity: What's on My head? Prop Story

What's on My Head? by Margaret Miller. New York: Little Simon, 2009.

Gather the photographed items from Miller's book—fireman's hat, stuffed puppy, plush frog, bow, fancy hat, rubber ducky—and place them in a brown bag. Pull each item out of the bag and place it on your head. Ask the children, "What's on my head?" If group is small and cooperative you can hold each item over a child's head and ask the question. After using the props, bring out the board book and invite the children to "read" the words along with you.

Music & Movement

Sound recording: track 15, "Snow Fun." *Preschool Action Time: Activities and Finger Plays* by Carole Hammett. Long Branch, NJ: Kimbo Educational, 1988, compact disc.

- Pretend to ice skate, throw snow balls, climb the slopes, and so on. When the snow is falling, make fingers flutter toward the ground like falling snowflakes.

Transition 2: I Can Wiggle

(Wiggle each body part.)
I can wiggle my fingers,
I can wiggle my toes.
I can wiggle my shoulders,
And I can wiggle my nose.
I can wiggle the wiggles
All out of me. *(wiggle whole body robustly)*
And I can sit
As still as can be. *(sit down and fold hands)*

Book 3

One Mitten by Kristine O'Connell George. New York: Clarion Books, 2004.
  - A lost mitten is found, so it is time to go outside and play.

Closing

ALTERNATIVE TITLES FOR WINTER CLOTHES: HATS AND MITTENS

Brett, Jan. *The Mitten: A Ukrainian Folktale.* New York: Putnam, 1989.

Carlstrom, Nancy White. *Jesse Bear, What Will You Wear?* New York: Macmillan ; London: Collier Macmillan, 1986.

Chodos-Irvine, Margaret. *Ella Sarah Gets Dressed.* San Diego, CA: Harcourt, 2003.

Greenstein, Elaine. *One Little Lamb.* New York: Viking, 2004.

Kellogg, Steven. *The Missing Mitten Mystery.* New York: Dial Books, 2000.

Kuskin, Karla. *Under My Hood I Have a Hat.* New York: Laura Geringer Books, 2004.

Low, Alice. *Aunt Lucy Went to Buy a Hat.* New York: HarperCollins, 2004.

Siddals, Mary McKenna. *Millions of Snowflakes.* New York: Clarion Books, 1998.

Wells, Rosemary. *Red Boots.* Baby Max and Ruby series. New York: Viking, 2009.

Spring, Week 1

Easter and Bunnies

Opening

Book 1

Wake Up, It's Spring! by Lisa Campbell Ernst. New York: HarperCollins, 2003.
- The arrival of spring is cause for celebration for an earthworm, a seed, and the rest of the world.

Interactive Activity: Ten Little Easter Bunnies Magnet Board

Download pattern 2.21 at alaeditions.org/webextras.

Ten little Easter bunnies with Easter eggs so fine,
One hopped away and then there were nine.

Nine little Easter bunnies standing up so straight,
One hopped away and then there were eight.

Eight little Easter bunnies as white as clouds in heaven,
One hopped away and then there were seven.

Seven little Easter bunnies with baskets made of sticks.
One hopped away and then there were six.

Six little Easter bunnies hoppy and alive,
One hopped away and then there were five.

Five little Easter bunnies with colorful baskets from the store,
One hopped away and then there were four.

Four little Easter bunnies out in the yard so free,
One hopped away and then there were three.

Three little Easter bunnies with bow ties brand-new,
One hopped away and then there were two.

Two little Easter bunnies enjoying the spring sun,
One hopped away and then there was one.

One little Easter bunny, ready for Easter fun,
She hopped away and then there were none.

Music & Movement

Sound recording: track 4, "Hop Like a Bunny." *Toddlers on Parade: Musical Exercises for Infants and Toddlers* by Carol Totsky Hammett. Long Branch, NJ: Kimbo Educational, 1985, compact disc.

- Perform the animal actions as they are named.

Transition 1: Open, Shut Them

(On "open," place both hands in front of you, palms facing away and open them wide. On "shut them," clench hands into fists.)
Open, shut them,
Open, shut them,
Give a little clap.
Open, shut them,
Open, shut them,
Put them in your lap. *(fold hands and put them in your lap)*

(Starting at the tummy, slowly "creep" fingers up toward the face.)
Creep them, creep them,
Slowly creep them,
Right up to your chin.
Open up your little mouth, *(open up your mouth)*
But do not let them in.
  (just as it looks like you're going to put fingers into mouth, quickly run fingers back down body toward tummy)

Falling, falling
Nearly to the ground, *(bend over and try to touch ground)*
Reach up your little arms *(reach arms up and stand on tiptoes)*
And shake them all around. *(shake arms over head)*

(Repeat first verse.)

Book 2

Spot's First Easter by Eric Hill. New York: G. P. Putnam's, 1988.
- Spot the puppy searches for six hidden Easter eggs. Flaps conceal where the eggs are hidden.

Interactive Activity: B-U-N-N-Y Flannelboard

Change the B-I-N-G-O song to the B-U-N-N-Y song. As you sing the song, remove the felt circle with the letter on it when the lyrics drop the letter. "There was a farmer who had a pet and Bunny was his name-o. *(clap)*-U-N-N-Y" and remove the *B*.

Music & Movement

Sound recording: track 8, "Bunny Hop." *Hunk-ta-bunk-ta Wiggle: Volume One: 12 Tunes for Toddlers* by Katherine Dines. Denver, CO: Hunk-Ta-Bunk-Ta Music, 2006, compact disc.
- Hop each time the word *hop* is sung. Then wiggle body parts as directed.

Transition 2: Clap Your Hands

(Follow motions described.)
Clap your hands, clap your hands,
Clap them just like me.
Touch your shoulders, touch your shoulders,
Touch them just like me.
Tap your knees, tap your knees,
Tap them just like me.
Shake your head, shake your head,
Shake it just like me.
Clap your hands, clap your hands,
Then let them quiet be. *(sit and fold hands in lap)*

Book 3

Bunny and Me by Adele Aron Greenspun. New York: Scholastic, 2000.
- Simple text and photographs portray a baby and a bunny playing together.

Closing

ALTERNATIVE TITLES FOR EASTER AND BUNNIES

Bridwell, Norman. *Clifford's First Easter.* New York: Scholastic, 1995.

Chalmers, Mary. *Easter Parade.* New York: Harper & Row, 1988.

Church, Caroline Jayne. *Here Comes Easter!* New York: Cartwheel Books, 2010.

Colandro, Lucille. *There Was an Old Lady Who Swallowed a Chick.* New York: Cartwheel Books, 2009.

Henkes, Kevin. *Little White Rabbit.* New York: Greenwillow Books, 2011.

Hulme, Joy N. *Easter Babies: A Springtime Counting Book.* New York: Sterling, 2010.

McCue, Lisa. *Quiet Bunny's Many Colors.* New York: Sterling Publishing Company, 2010.

Mortimer, Anne. *Bunny's Easter Egg.* New York: Katherine Tegan Books, 2010.

Park, Linda Sue. *What Does Bunny See? A Book of Colors and Flowers.* New York: Clarion Books, 2005.

Peters, Lisa Westberg. *We're Rabbits.* Orlando, FL: Harcourt, 2004.

Schulman, Janet. *10 Easter Egg Hunters.* New York: Alfred A. Knopf, 2010.

———. *Countdown to Spring: An Animal Counting Book.* New York: Alfred A. Knopf, 2002.

Stiegemeyer, Julie. *Seven Little Bunnies.* Tarrytown, NY: Marshall Cavendish, 2010.

Thompson, Lauren. *Wee Little Bunny.* New York: Simon & Schuster Books for Young Readers, 2010.

Weeks, Sarah. *Bunny Fun.* Orlando, FL: Harcourt, 2008.

ALTERNATIVE RHYME WITH MONKEY MITT

Five Little Rabbits

(As you count, add rabbit to your monkey mitt. Wiggle each finger and make motions with the rabbits. Insert your own name in the last verse.)
One little rabbit, not much fun.
He doesn't hop, he doesn't run.
Two little rabbits come out to play.
They hop a little then run away.
Three little rabbits, playing tag.
They hop in and out of an old trash bag.

(continued)

Four little rabbits, having quite a time.
They hop about, listening to *(your name)*'s rhyme.
Five little rabbits, each goes thump.
They hop through the garden. Watch them jump!

Spring, Week 2

Flowers

Opening

Book 1

Grow Flower, Grow! by Lisa Bruce. Originally titled *Fran's Flower*. New York: Scholastic, 2001.

- Fran has found a flowerpot and is determined to make its contents grow. Her patience wears thin, and she throws the pot out and eventually discovers a surprise.

Interactive Activity: Five Pretty Flowers Flannelboard

See page 83 for rhyme and pattern.

Music & Movement

Sound recording: track 6, "In My Garden." *One Light, One Sun* by Raffi. Willowdale, ON, Hollywood, CA: Troubadour Records, 1987, compact disc.

- Pretend to dig, hoe, plant, grow bigger, pick, and eat as directed by the song.

Transition 1: Open, Shut Them

(On "open," place both hands in front of you, palms facing away and open them wide. On "shut them," clench hands into fists.)
Open, shut them,
Open, shut them,
Give a little clap.
Open, shut them,

Open, shut them,
Put them in your lap. *(fold hands and put them in your lap)*

(Starting at the tummy, slowly "creep" fingers up toward the face.)
Creep them, creep them,
Slowly creep them,
Right up to your chin.
Open up your little mouth, *(open up your mouth)*
But do not let them in.
    (just as it looks like you're going to put fingers into mouth,
    quickly run fingers back down body toward tummy)

Falling, falling
Nearly to the ground, *(bend over and try to touch ground)*
Reach up your little arms *(reach arms up and stand on tiptoes)*
And shake them all around. *(shake arms over head)*

(Repeat first verse.)

Book 2

Bumblebee, Bumblebee, Do You Know Me? A Garden Guessing Game by Anne
F. Rockwell. New York: HarperCollins, 1999.
    - Riddles give descriptions of various flowers, then reveal their names.

Interactive Activity: Five Spring Flowers Flannelboard

Download pattern 2.22 a and b at alaeditions.org/webextras.

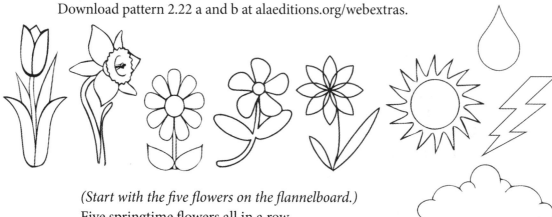

(Start with the five flowers on the flannelboard.)
Five springtime flowers all in a row.
The first flower said, "We need sunshine to grow."
The second flower said, "Oh my, we need water."
    (place raindrop above flower)

(continued)

The third flower said, "Yes, that sun is getting hotter."
   (place sun above flower)

The fourth flower said, "Could there be clouds in the sky?"
   (place cloud on board)
The fifth flower asked, "Hmmmm, I wonder why?"

Then, CRASH went the thunder and POW went the lightening.
   (place lightning bolt on board)
A rain storm sure sounds frightening.

Were the flowers worried?
No, no, no.
That beautiful storm helps them to
Grow, grow, grow!

Music & Movement

Sound recording: track 15, "The Flower Dance." *Let's Dance.* Burbank, CA: Walt Disney Records, 2010, compact disc.
   - Make your body loose and let your arms hang freely. Dance as if your arms are petals swaying in breeze.

Transition 2: Clap Your Hands

(Follow motions described.)
Clap your hands, clap your hands,
Clap them just like me.
Touch your shoulders, touch your shoulders,
Touch them just like me.
Tap your knees, tap your knees,
Tap them just like me.
Shake your head, shake your head,
Shake it just like me.
Clap your hands, clap your hands,
Then let them quiet be. *(sit and fold hands in lap)*

Book 3

Cimarusti, Marie Torres. *Peek-a-Bloom.* New York: Dutton Children's Books, 2010.
   - Lift-up flaps reveal rabbits, ducklings, flowers, and other signs of spring.

Closing

ALTERNATIVE TITLES FOR FLOWERS

Brenner, Barbara. *Good Morning, Garden*. Chanhassen, MN: NorthWord Press, 2004.

Ehlert, Lois. *Planting a Rainbow*. San Diego, CA: Harcourt Brace Jovanovich, 1988.

Greenstein, Elaine. *One Little Seed*. New York: Viking, 2004.

Kunhardt, Edith. *Judy's Flower Bed*. New York: Golden Books, 2005.

Park, Linda Sue. *What Does Bunny See? A Book of Colors and Flowers*. New York: Clarion Books, 2005.

Wellington, Monica. *Zinnia's Flower Garden*. New York: Dutton Children's Books, 2005.

Spring, Week 3

Food and Eating

Opening

Book 1

Sitting Down to Eat by Bill Harley. Little Rock, AR: August House Little Folk, 1996.

- A young boy agrees to share his snack with an ever-growing group of uninvited animals.

Interactive Activity: Five Tasty Sandwiches Magnet Board

Download pattern 2.23 at alaeditions.org/webextras.

(It's fun to use children's names on the verses and insert yourself into the last line.)
Five tasty sandwiches made of jelly and
  peanut butter.

(continued)

(Child's name) took one to share with his brother.
Four tasty sandwiches as peanutty as can be.
(Child's name) took one and now there are three.
Three tasty sandwiches made just for you.
(Child's name) took one and now there are two.
Two tasty sandwiches with jelly all nice and sweet.
(Child's name) took one for a story-hour treat.
How many sandwiches? Oh, no! We are left with just one.
(Your name) takes it—and now there are none.

Music & Movement

Sound recording: track 10, "Peanut Butter and Jelly." *Songs for Wiggleworms.*
Chicago, IL: Old Town School of Folk Music, 2000, compact disc.
- Follow the directions to crunch, squish, spread, and eat your sandwich.
Dance on "peanut, peanut butter, and jelly."

Transition 1: Open, Shut Them

*(On "open," place both hands in front of you, palms facing away and open
them wide. On "shut them," clench hands into fists.)*
Open, shut them,
Open, shut them,
Give a little clap.
Open, shut them,
Open, shut them,
Put them in your lap. *(fold hands and put them in your lap)*

(Starting at the tummy, slowly "creep" fingers up toward the face.)
Creep them, creep them,
Slowly creep them,
Right up to your chin.
Open up your little mouth, *(open up your mouth)*
But do not let them in.
    *(just as it looks like you're going to put fingers into mouth,
    quickly run fingers back down body toward tummy)*

Falling, falling
Nearly to the ground, *(bend over and try to touch ground)*
Reach up your little arms *(reach arms up and stand on tiptoes)*
And shake them all around. *(shake arms over head)*

(Repeat first verse.)

Book 2

Mouse Mess by Linnea Asplind Riley. New York: Blue Sky Press, 1997.
  - A hungry mouse leaves a mess behind as it searches for a snack.

Interactive Activity: The Food-Loving Lady Prop Story

Download patterns 2.24 a and b at alaeditions.org/webextras.

(Depending on the size of your group, the children
  can be given the "food" props to "feed" to the
  lady's stomach.)
Once there lived a food-loving lady
A fan of food, frosted or fried.
She loved all sorts of junk food
And never stopped eating to go outside.

With the TV on, she'd stay on her seat.
All day she was happy to just eat, eat, eat.
At one o'clock she ate a Big Mac.
At two o'clock she drank a soda six-pack.

At three o'clock she ate a chocolate bar.
At four o'clock she ate the cookies from the jar.
At five o'clock she ate a french fry.
At six o'clock she ate a cherry pie.

At seven o'clock she ate a bag of potato chips.
At eight o'clock she sucked some peppermint sticks.
At nine o'clock she had a hot dog on a bun.
At ten o'clock she enjoyed cotton candy—that's fun.

At eleven o'clock she ate a whole birthday cake.
And at twelve o'clock, that lady had a stomachache!

Music & Movement

Sound recording: track 17, "I Feel So Crazy I'll Jump in the Soup." *Victor Vito*
by Laurie Berkner. New York: Two Tomatoes, 1999, compact disc.

(Follow motions described.)
I feel crazy, so I jump in the soup.
I feel crazy, so I jump in the soup.

(continued)

I feel crazy, so I jump in the soup.
I jump, jump, jump, in the soup.

I feel crazy, so I swim in the soup . . .
I feel crazy, so I gallop in the soup . . .
I feel crazy, so I splash in the soup . . .
I feel crazy, so I sit in the soup . . .

Transition 2: Clap Your Hands

(Follow motions described.)
Clap your hands, clap your hands,
Clap them just like me.
Touch your shoulders, touch your shoulders,
Touch them just like me.
Tap your knees, tap your knees,
Tap them just like me.
Shake your head, shake your head,
Shake it just like me.
Clap your hands, clap your hands,
Then let them quiet be. *(sit and fold hands in lap)*

Book 3

The Little Mouse, the Red Ripe Strawberry, and the Big Hungry Bear by Don Wood. New York: Child's Play (International), 1984.
    - A little mouse tries to protect his strawberry from a big, hungry bear.

Closing

ALTERNATIVE TITLES FOR FOOD AND EATING

Barbour, Karen. *Little Nino's Pizzaria.* San Diego, CA: Harcourt Brace Jovanovich, 1987.

Carle, Eric. *Today Is Monday.* New York: Philomel Books, 1993.

Fleming, Denise. *Lunch.* New York: Henry Holt, 1992.

Goldstone, Bruce. *The Beastly Feast.* New York: Henry Holt, 1998.

McFarland, Lyn Rossiter. *Mouse Went Out to Get a Snack.* New York: Farrar Straus Giroux, 2005.

Pelham, David. *Sam's Sandwich.* New York: Dutton Children's Books, 1990.

Salerno, Steven. *Harry Hungry.* Orlando, FL: Harcourt Inc, 2009.

Walter, Virginia. *"Hi, Pizza Man!"* New York: Orchard Books, 1995.

Wellington, Monica. *Pizza at Sally's.* New York: Dutton Children's Books, 2006.

Spring, Week 4

Frogs

Opening

Book 1

Faulkner, Keith. *The Wide-Mouthed Frog: A Pop-up Book.* New York: Dial Books for Young Readers, 1996.

- A wide-mouthed frog is curious about what other animals eat.

Interactive Activity: Four Little Froggies Monkey Mitt

(Start with four frogs on your monkey mitt. As the frogs leave, remove one from your mitt.)
Four little frogs out near the sea—
One went swimming, and then there were three.
Three little frogs said, "Should we go too?"
Only one jumped in the water, and then there were two.
Two little frogs hopping in the sun—
One jumped in, and then there was one.
One lonely frog thought, "Alone is no fun!"
He joined his friends in the water, and then there were none.

Music & Movement

Sound recording: track 11, "Can You Leap Like a Frog?" *Kids in Action* by Greg & Steve. Acton, CA: Greg & Steve Productions; New York: distributed by Youngheart Music, 2000, compact disc.

- Leap like frogs, crawl like cats, fly like birds, hop like bunnies, swing arms like elephant trunks, and swim like fish, as the lyrics suggest.

Transition 1: Open, Shut Them

(On "open," place both hands in front of you, palms facing away and open
them wide. On "shut them," clench hands into fists.)
Open, shut them,
Open, shut them,
Give a little clap.
Open, shut them,
Open, shut them,
Put them in your lap. *(fold hands and put them in your lap)*

(Starting at the tummy, slowly "creep" fingers up toward the face.)
Creep them, creep them,
Slowly creep them,
Right up to your chin.
Open up your little mouth, *(open up your mouth)*
But do not let them in.
    (just as it looks like you're going to put fingers into mouth,
    quickly run fingers back down body toward tummy)

Falling, falling
Nearly to the ground, *(bend over and try to touch ground)*
Reach up your little arms *(reach arms up and stand on tiptoes)*
And shake them all around. *(shake arms over head)*

(Repeat first verse.)

Book 2

Hop, Jump by Ellen Stoll Walsh. San Diego, CA: Harcourt Brace Jovanovich,
1993.
    - A frog bored with hopping discovers he likes to dance instead.

Interactive Activity: Five Green and Speckled Frogs Flannelboard

Download pattern 2.25 at alaeditions.org/webextras.

(Start with five frogs, bugs, and logs on the board.
    Remove them as they jump into the pool.)
Five green and speckled frogs
Sitting on a hollow log,
Eating some most delicious bugs.
Yum, yum!

One frog jumped in the pool
Where it was nice and cool.
Now there are only four speckled frogs.
Glub, glub!

Four green and speckled frogs . . .
Three green and speckled frogs . . .
Two green and speckled frogs . . .

One green and speckled frog
Sitting on a hollow log,
Eating some most delicious bugs.
Yum, yum!

The frog jumped in the pool
Where it was nice and cool.
Now there are NO speckled frogs,
Glub, glub!

Music & Movement

Sound recording: track 1, "What a Miracle." *Walter the Waltzing Worm* by Hap Palmer. Freeport, NY: Activity Records, 1982, compact disc.

> *(During the verses, the children sing each echoed phrase and follow the motions described. During the chorus of the song, the children clap along and sing as much as they can remember.)*

I have hands, I have hands,
Watch me clap, watch me clap.
Oh, what a miracle am I.
I have feet, I have feet,
Watch me stamp, watch me stamp.
Oh, what a miracle am I.

Chorus:
Oh, what a miracle, oh, what a miracle,
Every little part of me.
I'm something special, so very special,
There's nobody quite like me.

I have arms, I have arms,
Watch me swing, watch me swing.
Oh, what a miracle am I.

(continued)

I have legs, I have legs,
They can bend and stretch, they can bend and stretch.
Oh, what a miracle am I.
(Repeat chorus.)

I have a spine, I have a spine,
It can twist and bend, it can twist and bend.
Oh, what a miracle am I.
I have one foot, I have one foot,
Watch me balance, watch me balance.
Oh, what a miracle am I.
(Repeat chorus.)

Transition 2: Clap Your Hands

(Follow motions described.)
Clap your hands, clap your hands,
Clap them just like me.
Touch your shoulders, touch your shoulders,
Touch them just like me.
Tap your knees, tap your knees,
Tap them just like me.
Shake your head, shake your head,
Shake it just like me.
Clap your hands, clap your hands,
Then let them quiet be. *(sit and fold hands in lap)*

Book 3

Five Green and Speckled Frogs by Priscilla Burris. New York: Scholastic, 2002.
   - Five frogs eat bugs as they sit on a log. After their snack they jump into the pool until all are gone.

Closing

ALTERNATIVE TITLES FOR FROGS

Breen, Steve. *Stick.* New York: Dial Books for Young Readers, 2007.

Burns, Kate. *Jump like a Frog.* London: David & Charles Children's Books, 1999.

Mitton, Tony. *Down by the Cool of the Pond.* New York: Orchard Books, 2001.

Parenteau, Shirley. *One Frog Sang.* Cambridge, MA: Candlewick Press, 2007.

Thompson, Lauren. *Leap Back Home to Me.* New York: Margaret K. McElderry Books, 2010.

Yolen, Jane. *Hoptoad.* San Diego, CA: Silver Whistle/Harcourt, 2003.

ALTERNATE PUPPET/ACTIVITY RHYME

(Use this rhyme with a frog puppet or plush animal. Act words out with the puppet. Invite the children to stand and hop with you as you recite poem. Repeat several times until the children can also recite rhyme.)

Here is a frog, hippity-hop;

Watch him hop,

And now a stop.

Another hop,

And another stop.

Spring, Week 5

Gardening and Vegetables

Opening

Book 1

Growing Vegetable Soup by Lois Ehlert. San Diego, CA: Harcourt Brace Jovanovich, 1987.

- A father and child grow and gather the vegetables needed to make soup.

Interactive Activity: The Gardener Plants the Seeds Magnet Board

Download pattern 2.26 a and b at alaeditions.org/webextras.

(Can be sung to the tune of "The Farmer in the Dell." Place each magnet on the board as you sing the word all in capitals.)

The GARDENER plants the SEEDS

The gardener plants the seeds

(continued)

High-ho the derry-o,
The gardener plants the seeds.

The RAIN falls on the ground . . .
The SUN shines bright and warm . . .
The seeds begin to GROW . . .
VEGETABLES grow everywhere . . .

Music & Movement

Sound recording: track 29, "Flower Garden." *Piggyback Songs: Singable Poems Set to Favorite Tunes*. Long Branch, NJ: Kimbo, 1995, compact disc.

(Pretend to plant seeds.)
The gardener plants the seeds.
The gardener plants the seeds.
High-ho the derry-o,
The gardener plants the seeds.

The rain falls on the ground . . .
  (wiggle fingers as you raise and lower your arms)
The sun shines bright and warm . . .
  (make arms into circle over head and sway)
The seeds begin to grow . . .
  (crouch down and slowly stand up to tiptoes)
Flowers grow everywhere . . .
  (spread arms out wide and look around)

Transition 1: Open, Shut Them

(On "open," place both hands in front of you, palms facing away and open them wide. On "shut them," clench hands into fists.)

Open, shut them,
Open, shut them,
Give a little clap.
Open, shut them,
Open, shut them,
Put them in your lap. *(fold hands and put them in your lap)*

(Starting at the tummy, slowly "creep" fingers up toward the face.)
Creep them, creep them,
Slowly creep them,
Right up to your chin.

Open up your little mouth, *(open up your mouth)*
But do not let them in.
> *(just as it looks like you're going to put fingers into mouth,*
> *quickly run fingers back down body toward tummy)*

Falling, falling
Nearly to the ground, *(bend over and try to touch ground)*
Reach up your little arms *(reach arms up and stand on tiptoes)*
And shake them all around. *(shake arms over head)*

(Repeat first verse.)

Book 2

Mrs. McNosh and the Great Big Squash by Sarah Weeks. New York: HarperFestival/Laura Geringer Books, 2000.
  - Mr. McNosh grows a huge squash.

Interactive Activity: Out in the Garden Flannelboard

Download pattern 2.27 at alaeditions.org/webextras.

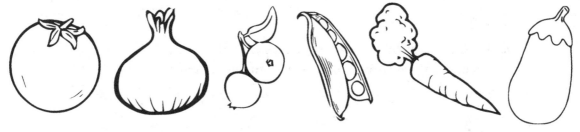

> *(Can be sung to the tune of "Down by the Station." Have enough vegetables*
> *for all children to handle one. After passing out the veggies, tell the chil-*
> *dren to listen for their turn to place a vegetable in the garden. After one*
> *"row" is complete, stop singing to count the item. Then remove the row*
> *and be ready for the next group.)*

Out in the garden, early in the morning,
See the red tomatoes all in a row.
See the proud gardener coming out to pick them.
Look, twist, pull, and off the tomato goes.

. . . yellow onions . . .
. . . blue berries . . .
. . . green pea pods . . .
. . . orange carrots . . .
. . . purple eggplant . . .

Music & Movement

Sound recording: track 14, "When the Pod Went Pop." *Sing a Song of Seasons* by Rachel Buchman. Cambridge, MA: Rounder Kids, 1997, compact disc.
- Instruct the children to act out what is happening to the peas. On *pop*, clap loudly.

Transition 2: Clap Your Hands

(Follow motions described.)
Clap your hands, clap your hands,
Clap them just like me.
Touch your shoulders, touch your shoulders,
Touch them just like me.
Tap your knees, tap your knees,
Tap them just like me.
Shake your head, shake your head,
Shake it just like me.
Clap your hands, clap your hands,
Then let them quiet be. *(sit and fold hands in lap)*

Book 3

The Surprise Garden by Zoe Hall. New York: Blue Sky Press, 1998.
- Three youngsters plant unidentified seeds and wait patiently for them to grow.

Closing

ALTERNATIVE TITLES FOR GARDENING AND VEGETABLES

Brenner, Barbara. *Good Morning, Garden.* Chanhassen, MN: North Word Press, 2004.

Brown, Ruth. *Ten Seeds.* New York: Knopf, 2001.

Ehlert, Lois. *Planting a Rainbow.* San Diego, CA: Harcourt Brace Jovanovich, 1988.

Evans, Lezlie. *The Bunnies' Picnic.* New York: Hyperion Books for Children, 2007.

Falwell, Cathryn. *Mystery Vine.* New York: Greenwillow Books, 2009.

Florian, Douglas. *Vegetable Garden.* San Diego, CA: Harcourt Brace Jovanovich, 1991.

Rosenberry, Vera. *Who Is in the Garden?* New York: Holiday House, 2001.

Urbanovic, Jackie. *Duck Soup.* New York: HarperCollins, 2008.

Spring, Week 6

Water and Rain

Opening

Book 1

Splish, Splash, Spring by Jan Carr. New York: Holiday House, 2001.
  - Rhyming text describes the wonders of spring.

Interactive Activity: Teddy Bear Flannelboard

Download pattern 2.28 a and b at alaeditions.org/webextras.

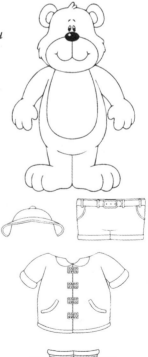

  (Start the story with the flannel bear on the board. As you sing the verses, dress the bear.)

One rainy morning, Teddy Bear watched the puddles in
  his front yard grow bigger and bigger.
"I want to jump in the puddles." Teddy told his mother.
"May I go outside and play in the rain?"

His mama said . . .
"Put on your hat, my buddy,
Put on your hat, my pet.
Put on your hat, my funny bear,
Or you will get wet."

Teddy put on his hat and said, "I'm going outside
  to jump in the puddles."
Then Mother Bear said,
"Put on your coat, my buddy,
Put on your coat, my pet.
Put on your coat, my silly bear,
Or you will get wet."

(continued)

And Teddy put on his raincoat.
"I am going out to play," announced Teddy Bear.
And Mother Bear said:
"Put on your boots, my buddy,
Put on your boots, my pet.
Put on your boots, my clever bear,
Or you will get wet."

So Teddy put on his boots.
"NOW, I am going outside to play in the puddles," he said.
And Mother Bear said, "Have fun, Teddy!"
Do you know what Teddy did then?
He went outside and splashed in every puddle.
And the best part is
Teddy didn't even get wet.

Music & Movement

Sound recording: track 8, "Ducks Like Rain." *H.U.M. All Year Long: Highly Usable Music Kids Can Sing, Dance & Do* by Carole Peterson. United States: Macaroni Soup, 2003, compact disc.

- Use duck sticks, waving them back and forth. Waddle around the room. On the quacks, stand still and quack.

Ducks like rain! Ducks like rain!
Ducks like splishy-splashing in the rain.
Ducks like rain! Ducks like rain!
Ducks like the rainy weather.
Water running off their feathers.
Ducks like splishy-splashing in the rain.
Quack quack quack quack quack
   (walk with a waddle, bottom stuck out behind you)
Quack quack quack quack quack
Quack quack quack quack quack
Quack! Quack! Quack!

Transition 1: Open, Shut Them

(On "open," place both hands in front of you, palms facing away and open them wide. On "shut them," clench hands into fists.)

Open, shut them,
Open, shut them,
Give a little clap.
Open, shut them,
Open, shut them,
Put them in your lap. *(fold hands and put them in your lap)*

(Starting at the tummy, slowly "creep" fingers up toward the face.)
Creep them, creep them,
Slowly creep them,
Right up to your chin.
Open up your little mouth, *(open up your mouth)*
But do not let them in.
  (just as it looks like you're going to put fingers into mouth, quickly run fingers back down body toward tummy)

Falling, falling
Nearly to the ground, *(bend over and try to touch ground)*
Reach up your little arms *(reach arms up and stand on tiptoes)*
And shake them all around. *(shake arms over head)*

(Repeat first verse.)

Book 2

It Looked Like Spilt Milk by Charles Green Shaw. New York: HarperCollins, 1947.
  - Illustrations convey some shapes that can be imagined in clouds.

Interactive Activity: My Umbrella Flannelboard

Based on the book *My Red Umbrella* by Robert Bright.
New York: William Morrow & Company, 1959.
- Download patterns 2.29 a and b at alaeditions.org/webextras.

(Place umbrella on board to start story.)
I shouldn't have bothered to bring my red umbrella.
It's a beautiful spring day.
But you never can tell when there may be a spring shower.
Just like that, here comes the rain.

(Place cloud on board. Place each animal on the board as they are named. If you have enough flannel animals for each child, they may assist in placing the animals on the flannelboard.)

And,
Here's a little dog to walk with me under my big umbrella.
And two kittens,
And three ducks,
And four little bunnies,
And a white bird,
And two butterflies.
We all fit under my big umbrella!

I wish we could make the rain stop.
Maybe if we all sing together . . . *(sing "Rain, rain, go away . . .")*
The rain has stopped!
   (place sun on board and remove animals as you name them)
And the two butterflies and the white bird can fly home.
Now the four little rabbits and the three ducks head home.
Finally the two little kittens and the red dog go home.
And I go home too with my big umbrella.
I think it's a good thing I brought it!

Music & Movement

Sound recording: track 8, "I Hear Thunder." *Wiggle and Whirl, Clap and Nap* by Sue Schnitzer. Boulder, CO: Weebee Music, 2005, compact disc.

- Use with rhythm instruments or egg shakers. When the song talks about thunder, play instruments loudly to rhythm. When it is raining, play softly.

Transition 2: Clap Your Hands

(Follow motions described.)
Clap your hands, clap your hands,
Clap them just like me.
Touch your shoulders, touch your shoulders,
Touch them just like me.
Tap your knees, tap your knees,
Tap them just like me.
Shake your head, shake your head,
Shake it just like me.
Clap your hands, clap your hands,
Then let them quiet be. *(sit and fold hands in lap)*

Book 3

What Color Was the Sky Today? by Miela Ford. New York: Greenwillow Books, 1997.

- Illustrations demonstrate the different color a sky can be as the weather changes.

Closing

ALTERNATIVE TITLES FOR WATER AND RAIN

Asch, Frank. *Water.* San Diego, CA: Harcourt Brace, 1995.

Beaumont, Karen. *Move Over, Rover!* Orlando, FL: Harcourt, 2006.

Carle, Eric. *Little Cloud.* New York: Philomel Books, 1996.

Colborn, Mary Palenick. *Rainy Day Slug.* Seattle, WA: Sasquatch Books, 2000.

Huntington, Amy. *One Monday.* New York: Orchard Books, 2001.

Locker, Thomas. *Cloud Dance.* San Diego , CA: Silver Whistle/Harcourt, 2000.

Root, Phyllis. *Soggy Saturday.* Cambridge, MA: Candlewick Press, 2001.

Summer, Week 1

Bath Time

Opening

Book 1

King Bidgood's in the Bathtub by Audrey Wood. San Diego, CA: Harcourt Brace Jovanovich, 1985.

> - A partying king refuses to get out of the bathtub to rule his kingdom.

Interactive Activity: Harley's Colorful Day Flannelboard

Based on the book *Dog's Colorful Day: A Messy Story about Colors and Counting* by Emma Dodd. New York: Dutton Children's Books, 2000.

> - See page 62.

Music & Movement

Sound recording: track 20, "Boogie Woogie Wash Rag Blues." *Peek-a-Boo: And Other Songs for Young Children* by Hap Palmer. Topanga, CA: Hap-Pal Music, 1997, compact disc.

> - Use with scarves. (Tissues may be used if scarves aren't available.) Pretend the scarves are washcloths and wash each body part as the song directs.

Transition 1: Wiggle Worms

> Once there were some little worms,
> And all they did was squirm and squirm.
> They wiggled and wiggled up and down,
> They wiggled and wiggled all around.
> They wiggled and wiggled and wiggled until
> They were tired and could sit very still. (have children sit down)
> Now they could listen.
> Now they could see.
> All the things
> I have here with me. *(start your storytime activity)*

Book 2

Big Red Tub by Julia Jarman. New York: Orchard Books, 2004.
   - A variety of animals join Stan and Stella in their bathtub for an adventure.

Interactive Activity: Mrs. McFancy and Her Wash Prop Story

Based on the book *Mrs. McNosh Hangs Up Her Wash* by Sarah Weeks. New York: HarperCollins, 1998.
   - Download patterns 2.30 a, b, c, and d at alaeditions.org/webextras.

*(The numbers indicate which items to hang on the line. Hang a clothesline
   across the story room. Hang each
   laminated item by a clothespin as the story is read.)*

Monday morning, Mrs. Nancy McFancy (1) brings out
   a tub (2) to do the wash.
She works all morning to hang what is wet on the
   clothesline to dry.
She hangs up the dresses (3). She hangs up the shirts (4).
She hangs up the underwear (5), hangers (6) and skirts (7).

She hangs up the socks (8). She hangs up the shoes (9).
She washes the paper and hangs up the news (10).
She hangs up dog (11) and his bowl (12) and his bone (13).
She uses her cell then hangs up the phone (14).

She hangs up a hat (15) and an old prom gown (16).
Two bats fly by (17) and she hangs them upside down.
She hangs up her coffee mug (18) and an old Christmas wreath (19).
She hangs up the brush she uses on teeth (20).

She hangs up her cat by the tip of its tail (21).

The mail man arrives, and she hangs him with the mail (22).

She takes off her gloves (23) and for a snack grabs a pear (24).

Then Mrs. Nancy McFancy hangs up HERSELF (1) beside her favorite chair. (25)

Music & Movement

Sound recording: track 5, "Wiggy Wiggles Freeze Dance." *Two Little Sounds: Fun with Phonics and Numbers* by Hap Palmer. Topanga, CA: Hap-Pal Music, 2003, compact disc.

   - See page 65.

Transition 2: Hands at My Side

(Follow motions described.)

Sometimes my hands are at my side.

Then behind my back they hide.

Sometimes I wiggle my fingers so.

I shake them fast and shake them slow.

Sometimes my hands go clap, clap, clap!

Then I rest them in my lap. (sit and fold hands in lap)

Book 3

Ashman, Linda. *Rub-a-Dub Sub.* San Diego, CA: Harcourt, 2003.

   - A boy travels underwater in his bright orange submarine meeting friendly sea animals.

Closing

ALTERNATIVE TITLES FOR BATH TIME

Fox, Christyan. *Bathtime PiggyWiggy.* Brooklyn, NY: Handprint Books, 2001.

Goodman, Joan E. *Bernard's Bath.* Honesdale, PA: Boyds Mills Press, 1996.

Kay, Julia. *Gulliver Snip.* New York: Henry Holt and Company, 2008.

Noonan, Julia. *Bath Day.* New York: Scholastic, 2000.

Patricelli, Leslie. *Tubby.* Somerville, MA: Candlewick Press, 2010.

Roth, Carol. *Ten Dirty Pigs; Ten Clean Pigs.* New York: North-South Books, 1999.

Segal, John. *Pirates Don't Take Baths.* New York: Philomel Books, 2011.

Wood, Don. *Piggies.* San Diego CA: Harcourt Brace Jovanovich, 1991.

Summer, Week 2

Bugs

Opening

Book 1

Kitten's Big Adventure by Mie Araki. Orlando, FL: Gulliver Books, Harcourt, 2005.

- A kitten tries to chase a butterfly but runs to his mama when the butterfly chases him.

Interactive Activity: Bug in a Rug Magnet Board

Download patterns 2.31 a and b at alaeditions.org/webextras.

(When storytime starts, have all the bugs displayed around the rug on your magnet board. When you reach this rhyme, take the bugs off. Take turns hiding one bug at a time under the rug. Ask the children to remember which bug is hiding.)

Bug in the rug,
Bug in the rug,
Which bug is under my rug?

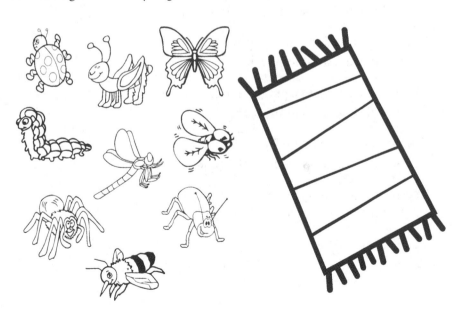

Music & Movement

Sound recording: disk 3, track 19, "The Ants Go Marching." *100 Sing-Along-Songs for Kids* by Cedarmont Kid Singers. Franklin, TN, 2007, compact disc.

(Use with rhythm sticks. Have the group form a circle or a single-file line. Lead the march in "follow the leader" fashion, keeping time with the rhythm sticks.)

The ants go marching one by one, hurrah, hurrah!
The ants go marching one by one, hurrah, hurrah!
The ants go marching one by one,
The little one stops to suck his thumb.
And they all go marching down to the ground
To get out of the rain—BOOM! BOOM! BOOM!

The ants go marching two by two . . .
    The little one stops to tie his shoe . . .

The ants go marching three by three . . .
    The little one stops to climb a tree . . .

The ants go marching four by four . . .
    The little one stops to shut the door . . .

The ants go marching five by five . . .
    The little one stops to take a dive . . .

The ants go marching six by six . . .
    The little one stops to pick up sticks . . .

The ants go marching seven by seven . . .
    The little one stops to pray to heaven . . .

The ants go marching eight by eight . . .
    The little one stops to shut the gate . . .

The ants go marching nine by nine . . .
    The little one stops to check the time . . .

The ants go marching ten by ten . . .
    The little one stops to say, "THE END!"

Transition 1: Wiggle Worms

Once there were some little worms,
And all they did was squirm and squirm.
They wiggled and wiggled up and down,
They wiggled and wiggled all around.
They wiggled and wiggled and wiggled until
They were tired and could sit very still. *(have children sit down)*
Now they could listen.
Now they could see.
All the things
I have here with me. *(start your storytime activity)*

Book 2

Foley, Greg E. *Don't Worry Bear* by Greg E. Foley. New York: Viking, 2008.
   - A caterpillar reassures Bear that they will see each other again when he comes out of his cocoon.

Interactive Activity: The Very Hungry Caterpillar Prop Story

The Very Hungry Caterpillar by Eric Carle. New York: Philomel Books, 1987.
   - Use with puppets and laminated foods. Tell the story with the caterpillar puppet nibbling through the foods. Print and enlarge the pictures from http://clubs-kids.scholastic.co.uk/clubs_assets/4630. After coloring, cut a circle about two inches in diameter through each piece. Write the text in permanent marker on the back of each laminated piece so you can easily tell the story. It is fun to have a butterfly puppet at the end if one is available. Be sure to show the children the book and explain that you retold the story from its original source.

Music & Movement

Sound recording: disk 3, track 2: "Baby Bumblebee." *100 Sing-Along-Songs for Kids* by Cedarmont Kid Singers. Franklin, TN: 2007, compact disc.

I'm bringing home a baby bumblebee, *(cup hand over other to hold bee)*
Won't my mommy be so proud of me,
I'm bringing home a baby bumblebee,
Ouch! It stung me! *(hold up index finger as if stung)*

I'm squishing up the baby bumblebee,
   (squish bee with thumb into palm of other hand)

(continued)

Won't my mommy be so proud of me,
I'm squishing up a baby bumblebee,
Ooh! It's yucky!

I'm wiping off the baby bumblebee, *(wipe hands on shirt)*
Won't my mommy be so proud of me,
I'm wiping off the baby bumblebee,
Now my mommy won't be mad at me!

Transition 2: Hands at My Side

(Follow motions described.)
Sometimes my hands are at my side.
Then behind my back they hide.
Sometimes I wiggle my fingers so.
I shake them fast and shake them slow.
Sometimes my hands go clap, clap, clap!
Then I rest them in my lap. (sit and fold hands in lap)

Book 3

Bugs! Bugs! Bugs! by Bob Barner. San Francisco, CA: Chronicle Books, 1999.
   - Rhyming text introduces children to familiar bugs.

Closing

ALTERNATIVE TITLES FOR BUGS

Carle, Eric. *The Very Busy Spider.* New York: Philomel Books, 1984.

Dodd, Emma. *I Love Bugs!* New York: Holiday House, 2010.

Durango, Julie. *Pest Fest.* New York: Simon & Schuster Books for Young Readers, 2007.

Finn, Isobel. *The Very Lazy Ladybug.* Wilton, CT: Tiger Tales, 1999.

Gershator, Phillis. *Zzzng! Zzzng! Zzzng! A Yoruba Tale.* New York: Orchard Books, 1996.

Koontz, Robin Michal. *Creepy Crawly Colors: A Pop-up Book.* New York: Little Simon, 2006.

Pedersen, Janet. *Houdini the Amazing Caterpillar.* New York: Clarion Books, 2008.

Stickland, Paul. *Big Bug, Little Bug.* New York: Scholastic. 2010.

Wilson-Max, Ken. *Lenny in the Garden.* London: Frances Lincoln Children's Books, 2009.

ALTERNATIVE MONKEY MITT

"There Was An Old Lady Who Swallowed a Fly"

Track 16: *More Silly Songs.* Burbank, CA: Walt Disney Records, 1998, compact disc.

- As you play the recording or recite the poem, place the puppets on a monkey mitt.

There was an old lady who swallowed a fly.
I don't know why she swallowed the fly,
I guess she'll die.

There was an old lady who swallowed a spider,
That wiggled and wiggled and tickled inside her.
She swallowed the spider to catch the fly.
I don't know why she swallowed the fly.
I guess she'll die.

There was an old lady who swallowed a bird.
How absurd to swallow a bird . . .

There was an old lady who swallowed a cat.
Imagine that, she swallowed a cat . . .

There was an old lady who swallowed a dog.
What a hog, to swallow a dog . . .

There was an old lady who swallowed a cow.
I don't know how she swallowed a cow . . .

I know an old lady who swallowed a horse.
She's dead, of course!

Summer, Week 3

Construction and Tools

Opening

Book 1

Construction Countdown by K. C. Olson. New York: Henry Holt, 2004.
  - The reader counts down construction equipment from 10 to 1.

Interactive Activity: Five Little Nails Flannelboard

Download pattern 2.32 at alaeditions.org/webextras.

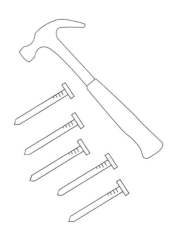

> *(Encourage the children to clap, tap, or pound
>   the ground with you on "Bam! Bam! Bam!")*

Five little nails
Standing straight and steady.
Here comes the carpenter
With a hammer ready!
Bam! Bam! Bam! *(remove one nail)*

Four little nails . . .
Three little nails . . .
Two little nails . . .
One little nail . . .

Music & Movement

Sound recording: track 4, "I Can Work with One Hammer." *Fun and Games: Learning to Play, Playing to Learn* by Greg & Steve. Acton, CA: Greg & Steve Productions, 2002, compact disc.

Johnny works with one hammer, one hammer, one hammer
  (hammer one fist lightly on leg)
Johnny works with one hammer
Then he works with two. *(hammer both fists on legs)*

Johnny works with two hammers . . . Then he works with three.

 (hammer both fists on legs and one foot on the floor)

Johnny works with three hammers . . . Then he works with four.

 (hammer both fists on legs and both feet on the floor)

Johnny works with four hammers . . . Then he works with five.

 (hammer both fists on legs, both feet on floor, and nod head down and up)

Johnny works with five hammers . . . Then he goes to sleep.

 (rest head on joined palms, pretending to go to sleep)

Transition 1: Wiggle Worms

Once there were some little worms,

And all they did was squirm and squirm.

They wiggled and wiggled up and down,

They wiggled and wiggled all around.

They wiggled and wiggled and wiggled until

They were tired and could sit very still. *(have children sit down)*

Now they could listen.

Now they could see.

All the things

I have here with me. *(start your storytime activity)*

Book 2

Get to Work, Trucks! by Don Carter. Brookfield, CT: Roaring Brook Press, 2002.

 - The reader follows a typical day of some working trucks.

Interactive Activity: Wheels on the Bus Flannelboard

(Place flannel pieces on the board as you sing the poem together with the children. Encourage the children to sing traditional verses as well as to make up some new ones.)

The wheels on the bus go round and round, (roll hands over each other)

Round and round, round and round.

The wheels on the bus go round and round

All through the town.

The driver on the bus says, "Move on back" . . .

 (put thumb up and throw it over your shoulder)

The wipers on the bus go swish, swish, swish . . .

 (put arms together in front of you and swish like windshield wipers)

The door on the bus goes open and shut . . .
   (cover eyes with hands on shut and uncover them on open)

The horn on the bus goes beep, beep, beep . . .
   (pretend to honk horn)

The baby on the bus says, "Wah, wah, wah!" . . .
   (put fisted hands in front of eyes and rub them like baby crying)

The people on the bus say, "Shh, shh, shh" . . .
   (put index finger to mouth on shh)

The mommy on the bus says, "I love you" . . .
   (point to self on I, put right hand over heart on "love," and point to others on "you.")

Music & Movement

Sound recording: track 11, "Bean Bag Rock"
Action Songs for Preschoolers: A Treasury of Fun by Georgiana Stewart. Long Branch, NJ: Kimbo Educational, 2003, compact disc.
   Use with beanbags, shaking them to the rhythm of the song. Balance the beanbags on body parts as the singer instructs.

Transition 2: Hands at My Side

(Follow motions described.)
Sometimes my hands are at my side.
Then behind my back they hide.
Sometimes I wiggle my fingers so.
I shake them fast and shake them slow.
Sometimes my hands go clap, clap, clap!
Then I rest them in my lap. *(sit and fold hands in lap)*

Book 3

I Love Tools by Philemon Sturges. New York: HarperCollins, 2006.
   - Children use a variety of tools to make a birdhouse.

Closing

ALTERNATIVE TITLES FOR CONSTRUCTION AND TOOLS

Augarde, Steve. *The New Yellow Bulldozer.* Brooklyn, NY: Ragged Bears, 2003.

Barton, Byron. *Machines at Work.* New York: Crowell, 1987.

London, Jonathon. *A Truck Goes Rattley-Bumpa.* New York: Henry Holt and Company, 2005.

Meltzer, Lynn. *The Construction Crew.* New York: Henry Holt & Company LLC, 2011.

McMullan, Kate. *I'm Dirty!* New York: Joanna Cotler Books, 2006.

Shulman, Lisa. *Old MacDonald Had a Woodshop.* New York: G. P. Putnam's Sons, 2002.

Stoeke, Janet Morgan. *Minerva Louise and the Red Truck.* New York: Dutton Children's Books, 2002.

Summer, Week 4

Fish and Fishing

Opening

Book 1

Splash by Ann Jonas. New York: Greenwillow Books, 1995.

- Readers answer the question "How many are in the pond?" as the animals jump in and out.

Interactive Activity: The Circle of Life Flannelboard

Sound Recording: track 5, "The Circle of Life." *Fins and Grins* by Johnette Downing. New Orleans, LA: Wiggle Worm Records, 2006, compact disc.

- Download patterns 2.33 a and b at alaeditions.org/webextras.

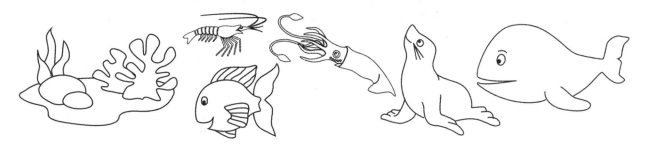

- Place the items on the flannelboard as they are mentioned in the song "The Circle of Life." Encourage the children to sing the echoes.

There is a sea, *(echo)*
The finest sea *(echo)*
That you ever did see. *(echo)*
And the circle of life goes around and around,
And the circle of life goes around.

And in that sea *(echo)*
There are some plants, *(echo)*
The finest plants *(echo)*
That you ever did see. *(echo)*
Oh, the plants in the sea
And the circle of life goes around and around,
And the circle of life goes around.

Now near those plants *(echo)*
There are some krill, *(echo)*
The finest krill *(echo)*
That you ever did see. *(echo)*
Oh, the krill need the plants,
The plants in the sea,
And the circle of life goes around and around,
And the circle of life goes around.

. . . Now near that krill there is a fish . . .
. . . Now near that fish there is a squid . . .
. . . Now near that squid there is a seal . . .
. . . Now near that seal there is a whale . . .

Now near that whale *(echo)*
There are some plants, *(echo)*
The finest plants *(echo)*
That you ever did see. *(echo)*
Oh, the plants need the whale,
The whale in the sea,
And the circle of life goes around and around,
And the circle of life goes around.

Music & Movement

Sound recording: track 9, "Fish Dance." *Music Time* by Johnette Downing. New Orleans, LA: Wiggle Worm Records, 2005, compact disc.

- Dance pretending to be fish. Swim to the left, right, in circles and to the bottom as instructed.

Transition 1: Wiggle Worms

Once there were some little worms,
And all they did was squirm and squirm.
They wiggled and wiggled up and down,
They wiggled and wiggled all around.
They wiggled and wiggled and wiggled until
They were tired and could sit very still. *(have children sit down)*
Now they could listen.
Now they could see.
All the things
I have here with me. *(start your storytime activity)*

Book 2

Hooray for Fish! by Lucy Cousins. Cambridge, MA: Candlewick Press, 2005.

- Little Fish introduces his friends in his underwater home.

Interactive Activity: Goldfish Magnet Board

From *Ready-to-Go Storytimes: Fingerplays, Scripts, Patterns, Music, and More* by Gail Benton and Trisha Waichulaitis (Neal Schuman, 2003).

- Download pattern 2.34 at alaeditions.org/webextras.

(The fishbowl can be drawn on a clear transparency film. Hold the transparency over the magnet pieces to create the visual of a fish tank. Practice placement to assure all pieces fit in the fish bowl.)

Goldfish swim by the light of day, one red and one orange, some white and gray. *(place fish on board as their colors are named)*

When diving through tunnels, shells they pass, and they nibble on the seaweed-like grass. *(place tunnel, shells, and grass as each is named)*

As they slide through the water they pop every bubble, their home is safe and free from trouble. *(place bubbles randomly on board)*

It's like a dance when they flick a fin. Hey! Look!

They're going around their bowl again.

Music & Movement

Sound recording: track 31, "I'm a Fish." *Piggyback Songs: Singable Poems Set to Favorite Tunes.* Long Branch, NJ: Kimbo, 1995, compact disc.

I'm a little fishy,

I can swim. *(pretend to swim like a fish)*

Here is my tail, here is my fin. *(put one arm on hip, then then other)*

When I want to have fun with my friends,

I wiggle my tail and dive right in! *(wiggle and pretend to dive)*

Transition 2: Hands at My Side

(Follow motions described.)

Sometimes my hands are at my side.

Then behind my back they hide.

Sometimes I wiggle my fingers so.

I shake them fast and shake them slow.

Sometimes my hands go clap, clap, clap!

Then I rest them in my lap. *(sit and fold hands in lap)*

Book 3

Fish Eyes: A Book You Can Count On by Lois Ehlert. San Diego, CA: Harcourt Brace Jovanovich, 1990.

- A counting book demonstrating the types of fish one could be.

Closing

ALTERNATIVE TITLES FOR FISH AND FISHING

Andreae, Giles. *Commotion in the Ocean.* Waukesha, WI: Little Tiger Press, 1998.

Banks, Kate. *That's Papa's Way.* New York: Frances Foster Books, 2009.

Barroux. *My Goldfish.* Grand Rapids, MI: Eerdmans Books for Young Readers, 2006.

DiPucchio, Kelly. *Gilbert Goldfish Wants a Pet.* New York: Dial Books for Young Readers, 2011.

Hendra, Sue. *Barry, the Fish with Fingers.* New York: Alfred A Knopf, 2010.

Kranz, Linda. *You Be You.* Lanham, MA: Taylor Trade Publishing, 2011.

Pfister, Marcus. *Play with Rainbow Fish: A Deluxe Pop-up Book.* New York: North-South Books, 2009.

Seuss, Dr. *One Fish, Two Fish, Red Fish, Blue Fish.* New York: Beginner Books; distributed by Random House, 1960.

Stockdale, Susan. *Fabulous Fishes.* Atlanta, GA: Peachtree, 2008.

Summer, Week 5

Picnics

Opening

Book 1

We're Going on a Picnic by Pat Hutchins. New York: Greenwillow Books, 2002.
- Hen, Duck, and Goose cannot agree on where they should eat their picnic.

Interactive Activity: On a Picnic We Will Go Prop Story

Download patterns 2.35 a, b, and c at alaeditions.org/webextras.

(Sing to the tune of "Farmer in the Dell." Pass out all the picnic foods and give the children a moment to name their tasty treat. Then sing the song below until all the items are hanging around the basket on the magnet board. Instruct the children to listen for their food and skip to the board when it is called. If the group is large, you may need to pass out the pieces twice to assure all get a turn.)

On a picnic we will go.
On a picnic we will go.
Let's empty our basket out.
On a picnic we will go.
(Child's name) brought a *(food).*
(Child's name) brought a *(food).*
Let's empty our basket out.
On a picnic we will go.
(Continue with all children and picnic foods.)

Music & Movement

Sound recording: track 2, "Sticky Bubble Gum." Peterson, Carole. *Sticky Bubble Gum and Other Tasty Tunes: Sing Along, Dance Along, Do Along.* United States: Macaroni Soup, 2002, compact disc.

- Clap hands together from side to side and do what the song suggests. On *unstuck*, pull off hands and start clapping for the next verse.

Transition 1: Wiggle Worms

Once there were some little worms,
And all they did was squirm and squirm.
They wiggled and wiggled up and down,
They wiggled and wiggled all around.
They wiggled and wiggled and wiggled until
They were tired and could sit very still. *(have children sit down)*
Now they could listen.
Now they could see.
All the things
I have here with me. *(start your storytime activity)*

Book 2

The Beastly Feast by Bruce Goldstone. New York: Henry Holt, 1998.

   - Different animals bring unusual foods to share at a picnic.

Interactive Activity: Five Tasty Sandwiches Magnet Board

   - See page 85.

Music & Movement

Sound recording, track 10, "Peanut Butter and Jelly." *Songs for Wiggleworms.*
Chicago, IL: Old Town School of Folk Music, 2000, compact disc.

   - See pages 85–86.

Transition 2: Hands at My Side

(Follow motions described.)
Sometimes my hands are at my side.
Then behind my back they hide.
Sometimes I wiggle my fingers so.
I shake them fast and shake them slow.
Sometimes my hands go clap, clap, clap!
Then I rest them in my lap. *(sit and fold hands in lap)*

Book 3

Picnic by Emily Arnold McCully. New York: HarperCollins Publishers, 2003.

   - Little Mouse gets lost on his way to a family picnic.

Closing

ALTERNATIVE TITLES FOR PICNICS

Evans, Lezlie. *The Bunnies' Picnic.* New York: Hyperion Books for Children, 2007.

Hill, Eric. *Spot's First Picnic.* New York: G. P. Putnam's Sons, 1987.

Jarrett, Clare. *The Best Picnic Ever.* Cambridge, MA: Candlewick Press, 2004.

Kasza, Keiko. *Ready for Anything!* New York: G. P. Putnam's Sons, 2009.

Kennedy, Jimmy. T*he Teddy Bears' Picnic.* New York: Macmillan Publishing Co, 1989.

Summer, Week 6

Zoos

Opening

Book 1

From Head to Toe by Eric Carle. New York: HarperCollins, 1997.
- The reader is encouraged to mimic the movements of various animals.

Interactive Activity: Polar Bear, Polar Bear, What Do You Hear? Prop Story

Polar Bear, Polar Bear, What Do You Hear? by Bill Martin. New York: Henry Holt, 1991.
- From www.dltk-teach.com/books/brownbear/sequel.htm print, color, laminate, and tape onto a wide popsicle stick an animal mask so that you have one for every child. Write the text in permanent marker on the back of each laminated piece so you can tell the story easily. As the children hear their animal named in the story, they should stand up and make their animal noise.

Music & Movement

Sound recording: track 10, "Zoo." *Dragon Tunes.* Los Angeles, CA: Kid Rhino, 2001, compact disc.
- Make the animal actions and noises as they are sung.

Transition 1: Wiggle Worms

Once there were some little worms,
And all they did was squirm and squirm.
They wiggled and wiggled up and down,
They wiggled and wiggled all around.
They wiggled and wiggled and wiggled until

They were tired and could sit very still. *(have children sit down)*
Now they could listen.
Now they could see.
All the things
I have here with me. *(start your storytime activity)*

Book 2

Dear Zoo by Rod Campbell. New York: Four Winds Press, 1982.
  - A prospective owner rejects the choices of pets sent to him from the zoo.

Interactive Activity: Five Little Monkeys Monkey Mitt and Crocodile Puppet

  - See page 48.

Music & Movement

Sound recording: track 13, "Going to the Zoo." *Singable Songs for the Very Young* by Raffi. Cambridge, MA: Rounder, 1976, compact disc.
  - Alternate walking and jogging in place pretending to be on your way to the zoo. Act like monkeys and crocodiles when those verses are sung.

Transition 2 : Hands at My Side

(Follow motions described.)
Sometimes my hands are at my side.
Then behind my back they hide.
Sometimes I wiggle my fingers so.
I shake them fast and shake them slow.
Sometimes my hands go clap, clap, clap!
Then I rest them in my lap. *(sit and fold hands in lap)*

Book 3

Good Night, Gorilla by Peggy Rathmann. New York: Putnam, 1994.
  - A zookeeper is followed home by the zoo animals.

Closing

ALTERNATIVE TITLES FOR ZOOS

Degman, Lori. *1 Zany Zoo.* New York: Simon & Schuster Books for Young Readers, 2010.

OHora, Zachariah. *Stop Snoring, Bernard!* New York: Henry Holt and Company, 2011.

Redmond, E. S. *Felicity Floo Visits the Zoo.* New York: Candlewick Press, 2009.

Rose, Deborah Lee. *Birthday Zoo.* Morton Grove, IL: A. Whitman, 2002.

Smith, Danna. *Two at the Zoo.* New York: Clarion Books, 2009.

Tildes, Phyllis Limbacher. *Animals: Black and White.* Watertown, MA: Charlesbridge, 1996.

NOTES

1. R. Arnold, "Public Libraries and Early Literacy: Raising a Reader," *American Libraries* 34 (2003): 48–51.

2. "Repetitive Reading Helps Toddlers Learn," *Growing Your Baby*, www.growingyourbaby.com/2011/02/21/repetitive-reading-helps-toddlers-learn/, February 21, 2011.

Young Readers

Transitioning from Story Hour
to Book Discussion

TRADITIONAL LIBRARY PROGRAMS TARGETED TO THE EARLY ELEMENTARY school years focus on the librarian presenting stories to the children. Discussion groups where the children carry the responsibility of discussing a book previously read are usually reserved for grade four and higher. We think of book discussion groups for the middle school years when reading is a perfected skill. Emergent readers may not be strong readers, but they can still discuss books.

This chapter and this book club require a different approach to presenting a book discussion. Rather than focusing on the reading of the book, the focus is on the enjoyment that comes from reading. When presenting quality books through discussion, games, crafts, and puzzles, an appreciation for how story develops comes naturally and easily. A young readers' book club introduces children to the concept of reading for pleasure. Given the opportunity to express their opinions, children prove to be creative and thoughtful. Offering a book club for emerging and beginning readers makes sense. Offering an emerging readers' book club to children who are eager to read allows the librarian to capture an audience and start them on their lifelong journey of pleasure reading.

Schools have increasing difficulty in finding time for pleasure reading. Reading teachers are pressured by state tests and a full curriculum. This is the perfect niche for a public library. While school teaches the dissecting of plot, character, and setting, the public library can introduce the wonderful world of reading for enjoyment. Because the focus is on pleasure, the discussion questions do not have a right or wrong answer. The answers may not even be in the story. That is intentional. Children can read stories without the pressure of finding a correct answer. They can express their opinion and learn that the views of others are different. They can develop confidence in their own ability to use words and share feelings. They can gain even more confidence from participating in a grown-up activity. In sum, they experience a story through multiple senses without anxiety about the resulting test or teachers' judgments.

Howard Gardner, an American development psychologist and a professor of cognition and education at Harvard University in the Graduate School of Education, is best known for his theory of multiple intelligences. In 1983, he introduced a theory that the human mind possesses many forms of intelligence. He also proposed that one individual can be skilled in multiple intelligences.[1] He does not believe intelligence to be a single measurable entity. Instead, Gardner suggests that one individual's intelligence is made up of the following categories:

- Linguistic intelligence—sensitivity to spoken and written language
- Logical-mathematical intelligence—the ability to investigate and analyze logically and scientifically
- Musical intelligence—the capacity to recognize and compose musical elements
- Bodily-kinesthetic intelligence—using one's whole body to solve problems
- Spatial intelligence—recognizing patterns of space
- Interpersonal intelligence—understanding the motivations and intentions of others
- Intrapersonal intelligence—understanding of one's own feelings and motivations
- Naturalistic intelligence—the ability to notice and characterize features of the environment

Teachers traditionally attend to the first two intelligences. These intelligences are easily accommodated by educational curriculum and standardized testing. As informal educators, librarians can incorporate all the intelligences into their programming work. The book club recognizes that children think and learn in many ways. The book club activities take into consideration that children possess multiple intelligences and may be developing several intelligences simultaneously. The intelligences rotate into the programs to complement the stories.

Young readers are having so much fun with the activities; they do not notice that they are learning and developing multiple intelligences through books.

Preparation

This program requires advance registration. It also needs to be limited to twelve or fifteen children. This allows for the purchasing of supplies and allows every participant the opportunity to be heard. As children register for this program, it is imperative that the caregiver understands that the book for each week must be read before arriving at the library. Explain that the book will not be read during library time, as this is often contrary to previously attended storytimes. When registration is placed, the first week's title should be available for pickup. Keep the books at the children's reference desk so as to keep track of who has picked up the book. It is recommended that several days before the first meeting a reminder is given to families who registered but may not have picked up the book. A text or e-mail message will suffice, but you can reiterate the book's club purpose if you place a personal phone call. Parents also appreciate a reminder call to read the book to those children who already have the book in their possession.

Remind parents at registration and book pickup times that participants are not required to be "the reader." It is okay if parents read the book to the youngest participants. Caregivers often question if their nonreader will be asked to read while in the library. Reassure them that it is not a prerequisite and if needed, reading help is always offered. Families often share the book club title together. Family literacy is an unintended but positive outcome of this program. (An explanatory letter to provide to parents is offered in appendix D.)

The summer session offers three book clubs. Families often are eager to register for summer reading enrichment but cannot commit to a six-week program. By shortening the program to three weeks, the library can offer a summer program in two separate three-week sessions to serve a larger number of children. In the summer session, the age range best served by this program is the children entering grades one and two. When scheduling, a librarian may want to consider allowing a week or two between summer session 1 and summer session 2. The two weeks in between allow the library additional time to have the books from the first group of children returned and available to be checked out by the second.

The titles for weeks 2 through 6 (or, 2 and 3 in the summer) are available one week prior to discussion. Pass them out to caregivers for checkout at the end of each book club meeting. The circulation staff may appreciate having the books at the desk during the program for the adults to check out at their convenience. This alleviates the rush to the circulation desk when the 45-minute club ends. It is helpful to return any books that were not checked out to the children's reference desk. Absent participants can then pick up the book prior to the next meeting. Additionally, reminder phone calls can be placed if necessary. Keeping only one book in the participants' hands works better than checking out all six titles at the time of registration—the children do not feel overwhelmed. Additionally, the librarian maintains the flexibility to rearrange or change titles if necessary.

Each week the club follows the same structure:

1. Discussion time: 20 to 25 minutes
2. Game or physical activity: 5 to 10 minutes
3. Craft: 5 to 15 minutes
4. Wrap-up: 5 to 10 minutes (clean up supplies and pass out next book)

The children will begin book club by gathering on the floor and sitting in a circle. The discussion questions, written on laminated card stock and placed in a container of some sort, will be passed around the circle and will randomly "stop" at a child. Using music (as in musical chairs) is fun and excites the participants. Musical suggestions fit the theme of the book being discussed. However, any music will do. When the librarian stops the music, the child holding the container pulls out a question and reads it to the group. Allow tentative readers the opportunity to ask more confident readers to assist them. That child then has the first opportunity to answer the question. Again, if they are unsure or shy, they can choose a friend to answer instead. The librarian should collect each question discussed so it does not get returned to the container. Allow many children to answer each question. Feel free to answer the question as moderator too. But do not force any child to participate; often their discussion will occur before or after class and in their homes. There are more questions than time will allow, and it is likely that not all the questions will be discussed.

While the children arrive and are awaiting their friends, informal discussion often occurs. Engage early attendees with one-on-one conversation. You can talk individually about what they liked best about the week's book or which has been their favorite title so far. It is okay if a child dislikes the book. When children do not like a title, the discussion can be livelier. It is also natural to talk about how this story compares to other books they have read. The children's ideas that are shared during this informal time often help guide future activities and point the moderator toward other titles.

It is important to read the week's plan in advance for best arrangement of the activities. Some weeks there may be two steps to a craft, and "drying" time may need to be considered. Arrange the craft and game around such necessities. The material lists at the beginning of the chapter will help you gather supplies.

Allow for some silliness and alert the library staff that the children may become louder than those attending any of the other storytimes. This is true especially if there is a competitive game. Remind the children that they need to maintain an "indoor voice," but do not expect silence. They have left school and are having fun with books. Allow participants to loosen up a bit. The activities do address the multiple intelligences as well as enjoyment. It is rewarding for parents, library staff, and other library patrons to see the enthusiasm and delight in the children. Demonstrating that children can become excited with books at the library is an awesome message for everyone in the library to receive!

Plan ahead

- Six to eight weeks before your story term begins, gather or purchase the recommended materials. While some libraries have an established budget line to use for storytime and craft materials, others do not. If your budget does not allow, approach your Friends of the Library group or seek donations with administrative approval. Be mindful that many of the items purchased will be used in multiple sessions and for many years. Over time only the cost of the consumable materials will be necessary. When ordering, I suggest purchasing enough for sixteen children. See tables on pages 128 and 129.

Stock Supplies

- ☐ music player
- ☐ scissors
- ☐ paintbrushes
- ☐ crayons
- ☐ school glue
- ☐ construction paper (in a variety of colors)
- ☐ craft glue (tacky glue)

- ☐ markers
- ☐ fine-tip black permanent markers
- ☐ cellophane tape
- ☐ staplers
- ☐ hole punches
- ☐ sets of dice (ideally eight sets of two; available new at http://boardgamedesign.com)

Table 3.1
Winter Quarter Material Lists

CONSUMABLE SUPPLIES TO PURCHASE

☐ Large dog biscuits
☐ Small wiggly eyes
☐ Ribbon
☐ Black, brown, & pink felt
☐ Brown lunch bags
☐ Green Easter grass or confetti
☐ Paper plates
☐ Plastic bags
☐ Wheel shaped pasta
☐ Silver glitter
☐ Waxed paper
☐ White thread
☐ Pebbles
☐ Hairspray
☐ Rubber bands

REUSABLE ITEMS TO GATHER:

☐ 2 sets of costume jewelry, fancy accessories, high heels, tiaras
☐ 1 fancy hat
☐ 1 knit cap
☐ 2 empty boxes (copy paper size)
☐ 1 sewing box
☐ 2 button-down sweaters
☐ 1- or 2-quart cooking pot
☐ 1 clean pizza delivery box
☐ Cancelled magazines
☐ 2 plastic sleds with rope handle for pulling

Table 3.2
Spring Quarter Material Lists

CONSUMABLE SUPPLIES TO PURCHASE

☐ White business-sized envelopes
☐ Yarn (white)
☐ 1" Styrofoam balls
☐ ¼ inch buttons
☐ Ribbon
☐ Blue poster paint
☐ Toothpicks
☐ Cotton balls
☐ #2 pencils
☐ Circle sequins
☐ Brown grocery bags
☐ Raffia
☐ White pipe cleaners
☐ Nabisco Barnum's Animal Crackers (plain)

REUSABLE ITEMS TO GATHER:

☐ Dog bowl
☐ Rawhide bone
☐ Cardboard pieces
☐ Basket
☐ Stuffed animal pig
☐ Witch's hat
☐ Fish bowl (plastic)
☐ Popcorn tub
☐ "Chomp" card game (available for purchase at http://educationallearninggames.com
☐ Bingo dabbers

Table 3.3
Summer Quarter Material Lists

**CONSUMABLE SUPPLIES
TO PURCHASE**

- ☐ Wooden clothespins
- ☐ Green tempera paint
- ☐ White craft foam
- ☐ Small googly eyes
- ☐ 9" x 9" Styrofoam balls
- ☐ 11/16" safety pins
- ☐ 2" safety pins
- ☐ Green, red, and white seed beads
- ☐ Toilet paper
- ☐ Sandwich-size baggies
- ☐ Colored tissue paper
- ☐ Colored cellophane
- ☐ Green chenille stems

**REUSABLE ITEMS
TO GATHER:**

- ☐ 30 plastic Easter eggs
- ☐ Popcorn tub
- ☐ Butterfly net

Table 3.4
Fall Quarter Material Lists

**CONSUMABLE SUPPLIES
TO PURCHASE**

- ☐ Brown pipe cleaners
- ☐ Kraft Jet-Puff Mini-Marshmallows
- ☐ Liquid starch
- ☐ Colored tissue paper
- ☐ Paint brushes
- ☐ Black garbage bags
- ☐ Spangler Dum Dum Pops (Lollipops)
- ☐ Small straw hats
- ☐ Felt—orange, red, yellow, and brown
- ☐ Small googly eyes
- ☐ Orange chenille stems
- ☐ Popsicle sticks
- ☐ Orange poster board
- ☐ Orange acrylic paint
- ☐ Paper egg cartons
- ☐ Paper clips

**REUSABLE ITEMS
TO GATHER:**

- ☐ Apple bushel basket
- ☐ 2 plastic apples
- ☐ 16 margarine containers
- ☐ 5 lids plastic beverage bottles(colored)
- ☐ Witch's hat
- ☐ 2 buckets
- ☐ 2 sponges
- ☐ 2 yardsticks
- ☐ Plastic jack-o'-lantern
- ☐ 2 small pumpkins or gourds
- ☐ Bandana to use as blindfold

- If necessary, garage sales, rummage sales, and secondhand stores are useful in collecting the items six to eight weeks before your program begins. Try telling the seller that the item is being used in a library program. It might be worth a price break. It is often acceptable to request donations from local businesses and the participants' families. Check with your administration. Sending a friendly e-mail to colleagues often nets a large amount of your needed secondhand items as well. Appendix C contains a printable wish list for sharing with colleagues.
- One month before your programs begin, print out the patterns and make copies. Cut out the shapes and print the discussion questions onto them. Laminate for durability. If there is a central department that does duplication and lamination confirm that they can complete your materials in time.
- Assure that your titles are available in multiples, and allow enough time to obtain one copy of each title for every registered child.
- Two weeks before your programs begins, conduct registration. Check your registration—if siblings are registered you can order fewer copies of each book.
- Order any audio recordings needed for your programs. It is optional but interesting to have background music available for circle time. Confirm that your music player is operational. It is always wise to check cables, cords, speakers, batteries, plugs, and the track on the CD to make sure the one you need works! If you schedule equipment and meeting room space within the building, make sure what you need is scheduled for you, not someone else.
- One to two weeks before your program begins, make a sample of each craft and precut any craft pieces you will need.
- One to two days before you present your program, reread the book and questions. Gather all the game pieces, craft supplies, and sample craft.

Tips and Tricks

- Sit in the circle with the children and take your turn reading and answering questions. Children will see you as a fellow participant and not as a "teacher" looking for the "correct" answer.
- Remind children every week that they need to be respectful of everyone's opinion and that only one person can speak at a time.
- When the game or activity is a huge hit, feel free to repeat it. Occasionally you may want to offer a prize for game winners. Based on library

policy, offering a small piece of candy to eat *after* storytime or giving out a bookmark is appropriate. Having a lesser prize for nonwinners, such as a sticker, helps prevent hurt feelings.

- Allow the children to complete the crafts themselves without too much adult help. If the crafts do not look perfect, it is okay. The experience with the story is the priority. If the children become frustrated with their own crafting ability, suggest they ask a friend to help them. Faster crafters can also assist others when time is running short. Remind the children that the sample is not the only way to complete a project but simply an example to guide them.
- If possible, work toward owning a book club collection. Purchasing multiple copies of the books is justified, as the club will be offered again and each title will be used numerous times. Think about paperbacks in such cases. If the titles can be bar-coded and shelved off the floor, you will be assured that your titles will not be weeded. Recording by hand which participant has each book protects your collection if the books must be bar-coded as "Reference" or "In-Library Use Only."
- Store your book club materials together. Keeping extra copies, extra cutout materials, and the purchased items makes for an easy repetition of the program in subsequent years. Store items by book title.
- Mark off-floor shelving clearly so materials are not inadvertently discarded by other staff.
- Because the club is offered to three grades of children (kindergarten, first grade, and second grade), the titles will begin to repeat in a three-year cycle. Be strict with the grade requirement for participation in the club. Older children do not want to be with younger children. And, despite reading ability, preschoolers do not belong with older students. It is not about the reading ability but the social experience of talking and sharing. With strong-willed parents, remind them that the club cycles and their child can participate in the next go-round when the child is at the appropriate age.
- Ideally, the tables for craft should allow for the children to be facing one another. Keep open the atmosphere of sharing.
- As the children engage in the games and crafts, circulate around the room to assist the children and discuss their activities. Additional informal discussion of the book can take place.
- Prepare name tags so participants can become familiar with one another.
- Set the tone early that all answers are welcome. Thank children for their participation and create a mood of fun.
- Give everyone a chance to talk, and politely encourage long-winded

participants to speak long enough only to make one point. The first week this is not usually a problem. However, by week 6 most of the children have a lot to say!

- Stay on topic. Help guide the children's comments along the book's theme. Time is short, and there are lots of ideas to welcome into the conversations.

- Have fun—the depth of responses will delight! Jot down the creative, intelligent, and unexpected comments. Include them in your reports to your administration and in newsletters. Share them with parents. Those comments may prove useful in justifying future funding for your club.

Fall, Week 1

Apples to Oregon

Book

Hopkinson, Deborah. *Apples to Oregon: Being the (Slightly) True Narrative of How a Brave Pioneer Father Brought Apples, Peaches, Pears, Plums, Grapes, and Cherries (and Children) across the Plains.* New York: Atheneum Books for Young Readers, 2004.

- Follow Delicious's family as they travel from Iowa to Oregon in the 1800s. Laugh with Delicious and Papa as they relocate the precious fruit trees that accompany them in their wagon. In tall-tale format, the book concludes with a successful orchard planting in Oregon.

Musical Selection

Sound recording: track 6, "Oregon Trail." *Woody Guthrie Sings Folk Songs* by Woody Guthrie. Washington, DC: Smithsonian/Folkways. Cambridge, MA: Rounder Records, 1989, compact disc.

Questions

Print the following questions on an APPLE shape (download pattern 3.1 at alaeditions.org/webextras) and laminate them. Have an apple basket to place the questions in as they rotate around your discussion circle.

- What are some tough challenges you have faced?
- In what ways was the family rich?
- Would you have followed the gold rush after an already long journey?
- Did you like the title? Why or why not?
- After reading this story, do you think about the story of Johnny Appleseed in the same way?
- How would you have crossed the river?
- What is your favorite fruit?
- What do you think Delicious's brothers and sisters might have been named?
- Was there anything you found funny in the illustrations?
- Would you have been as brave as Delicious? Why or why not?
- What is a tall tale? Were any parts of this story like a tall tale?
- How does it feel when you see a daddy cry?
- What other things may have been transplanted into the West from the East?
- Do you have a special something that you would do anything to protect? What is it?
- What parts of the story did you know were NOT true?
- Do you have any fruit trees at home? What do you think needs to be done to take care of the trees?

Game (Choose One)

PASS THE APPLE GAME 1

- Play like hot potato. Have the children sit in a circle.
- Pass a plastic apple around the circle while music is playing.
- When the music stops, the child holding the apple sits in the middle of the circle until the music stops again. The next child replaces the first. Winner is the last child left with the apple.

PASS THE APPLE GAME 2

- Divide the children into two groups. Each team makes a single-file line.
- The first child holds a plastic apple under his chin and passes the apple to the next child in line without using his hands.
- The first team to pass the apple through all their members wins!

Craft: There's a Worm in My Apple

Download pattern 3.2 at alaeditions.org/webextras.

- Cut out one apple shape and one leaf per child.
- Use a hole punch to punch four holes in the apple.
- Color the apple red, yellow, or green.
- Weave a brown chenille stem through the holes.
- Glue on the leaf.

Materials

- discussion questions, cut and laminated
- audio CD and player
- apple bushel basket
- 2 plastic apples
- precut apple shapes and stems (1 per child)
- hole punches
- brown chenille stems
- scissors
- glue
- crayons or markers

Fall, Week 2

I Lost My Tooth In Africa

Book

Diakité, Penda. *I Lost My Tooth in Africa*. New York: Scholastic Press, 2006.
  - In West Africa, the tooth fairy doesn't bring coins but living, clucking chickens. Amina hopes to lose her own wiggly tooth when her family visits family in Mali, West Africa.

Musical Selection

Back to Africa by Mor Thiam. Montreal: Justin Time, 1999, compact disc.

Questions

Download pattern 3.3 at alaeditions.org/webextras.

Print the questions on a TOOTH shape and laminate them. Have a basket to place the questions in as they rotate around your discussion circle. If time allows, enlarge the mouth shape from Smiling Mouth craft below to turn your basket into a mouth for the children to reach into.

- What do you think the tooth fairy does with the teeth she collects?
- What is the longest trip you have taken?
- How do you think Amina felt as she said goodbye to her chickens?
- Tell about a time your tooth fell out.
- How does it feel to have a wiggly tooth?
- How would living in Africa be the same as living in America? How would it be different?
- Would you like to brush your teeth under a tree? Why or why not?
- When did Amina need to be patient?
- Why do you think a young girl would write this story down?
- Did you like the African words being mixed into the story? Why or why not?
- Would you prefer a chicken or a dollar from the tooth fairy? Why?
- Do you think Amina got her wish?

Game: Mini Marshmallow Tooth Game

- Divide the children into groups of 2, 3, or 4.
- Each child is given a game board and a Dixie cup of mini marshmallows (download pattern 3.4 at alaeditions.org/webextras).
- Children take turns rolling the die. Place the same amount of mini marshmallows on the game board as on the roll of the die.
- Play passes to next player.
- First player to cover all twenty teeth wins.

Craft: Smiling Mouth

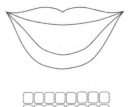

- Each child should cut a pair of smiling lips out of red construction paper and a bunch of teeth from white paper. Download pattern 3.5 at alaeditions.org/webextras.

- Glue the teeth onto the lips to make big toothy smiles. (Optional: Leave an open space for the tooth that fell out.)

Materials

- discussion questions, cut and laminated
- audio CD and player
- dice
- Campfire brand mini marshmallows
  Important: Recognizing that the health and safety of children is of the utmost importance, the foods listed in this resource are free of the most common four food allergens: eggs, peanuts, tree nuts, and milk. Deviating from the brand name will not assure allergen safety. For more information, see http://snacksafely.com/snackguide.
- Dixie cups to put the marshmallows in
- Tooth Game page for each player
- construction-paper lips
- white paper for teeth
- scissors
- glue

Reminder

Send home a note with children to bring in an empty glass jar for next week. (See appendix E.)

Fall, Week 3

Just a Dream

Book

Van Allsburg, Chris. *Just a Dream*. Boston: Houghton Mifflin, 1990.
- Young Walter doesn't understand the importance of caring for the environment. He takes an incredible journey through potential lands of the future. Will his adventures change his priorities? Or is it all just a dream?

Musical Selection

Amazon Rain Forest: Enhanced with Music. Chadds Ford, PA: Creative Music Marketing. Distributed by Valley Cottage, NY: Eclipse Music Group, 1996, compact disc.

Questions

Print the questions on a TREE shape and laminate them (download figure 3.6 at alaeditions.org/webextras). Have a recyclable container (such as an old margarine tub) to place the questions in as they rotate around your discussion circle.

- Would you like a tree for a birthday gift? Why or why not?
- How do we know Walter has changed?
- Could this story be true? Why or why not?
- Did you like Walter as a character before his dream? After his dream?
- How might the future be easier?
- Why do you think the author chose to have no words on some of the pages?
- What do you think Walter learned from his dreams?
- Did you see a future you liked in the story? If not, what kind of future would you like to live in?
- What do you think the future will be like?
- Could this story be told without the pictures? Why or why not?
- Have you ever had a dream change your mind about something?
- What else could you (or Walter) do to help the environment?

Game: Reduce, Reuse, Recycle Board Game

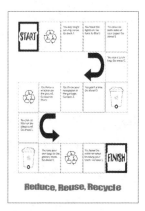

- Break the children into groups of two, three, or four. Each group will need the game board and a die for rolling (download figure 3.7 at ala editions.org/webextras). For markers, each child in the group may use a different color top from a two-liter bottle.
- Roll the die and move the correct number of spaces. Do as the board space tells.
- First child to reach the finish line wins!

Craft: Flower Vase

(This could also be a pencil holder, candy holder, or desk organizer. Reinforce the theme of recycling old trash and reusing the material to make something new. The finished product will depend on the glass each child brought from home.)

- Pour liquid starch into old margarine containers.
- Children cut or tear tissue paper into small pieces.
- Place a piece of tissue on the glass bottle and brush liquid starch over it. Repeat until the entire container is covered with tissue paper pieces. Overlapping creates a wrinkly effect.
- Let dry.

Materials

- discussion questions, cut and laminated
- audio CD and player
- large margarine container for passing questions
- small margarine containers for liquid starch (1 per child)
- game boards
- dice
- colored lids from plastic beverage bottles
- empty bottle or jar (must be glass)
- scissors
- different colors of tissue paper
- liquid starch
- paintbrushes

Fall, Week 4

Room on the Broom

Book

Donaldson, Julia. *Room on the Broom.* New York: Dial Books for Young Readers, 2001.

- A dog, frog, and parrot come to a witch's aid when the wind sends her hat, hair bow, and wand flying. In return they request a broom ride. Danger ensues when in flight they encounter a big, red dragon.

Musical Selection

Sound recording: track 9, "Witch Twitch." *Big Pumpkin* by Mr. Billy. WI: Doctors Orders Music, 2009, compact disc.

Questions

Print the questions on a WITCH HAT shape (download figure 3.8 at alaeditions.org/webextras) and laminate them. Have a witch hat to place the questions in as they rotate around your discussion circle.

- Have you ever taken a trip with a group of people?
- Do you ever need help finding your things? Who helps you?
- Where have you seen witches before?
- Is this a story for Halloween?
- Did you like the text rhyming? Why or why not?
- Have you ever joined forces with someone before? With whom, and why?
- Could the cat have scared off the dragon alone? Why or why not?
- Have you ever lost anything? What?
- Do you accomplish more on your own or with a group? Why?
- Is the witch in this story different or the same as other witches you have read about?
- Why do you think the author had the witch lose her broom?
- Do you think the witch and animals are friends? Why or why not?
- What do you think of when you hear the word *witch*?

Game: Melt the Witch

- Before the children arrive, draw two witch's heads on the chalkboard or dry erase board—one for each team of children.
- Fill two buckets with water and place a sponge in each.
- Divide children into two teams.
- Have children stand by the bucket (close enough to be able to accurately hit the board.)
- The children on each team take turns throwing the wet sponge at the witch. Important: Remind the children to wring out the sponges before throwing them. You may want to cut plastic garbage bags or use a tarp to cover the floor between the buckets and boards.
- The first team to completely "melt away" their witch wins!

Craft: Witch Sucker

- Download pattern 3.9 at alaeditions.org/ webextras.
- The children cut out two witch faces.
- Children color the faces.
- Put a small amount of glue on each face and stick it on the front and back of a lollipop or sucker.
- For the capes: cut a three-by-three-inch square, one per child, from a black garbage bag ; then cut the squares in half diagonally to make triangles.
- Each child tapes the garbage bag to their lollipop.

Materials

- discussion questions, cut and laminated
- audio CD and player
- witch hat
- 2 buckets
- 2 sponges
- chalkboard or dry erase board
- witch face pattern
- crayons or markers
- tape
- glue
- black garbage bags
- Spangler Dum Dum Pops (lollipops)

Important: Recognizing that the health and safety of children is of the utmost importance, the foods listed in this resource are free of the most common four food allergens: eggs, peanuts, tree nuts, and milk. Deviating from the brand name will not assure allergen safety. For more information, see http://snacksafely.com/snackguide.

Fall, Week 5

Thank You Sarah: The Woman Who Saved Thanksgiving

Book: Thank You, Sarah: The Woman Who Saved Thanksgiving

Anderson, Laurie Halse. *Thank You, Sarah: The Woman Who Saved Thanksgiving*. New York: Simon & Schuster Books for Young Readers, 2002.

- Sarah Hale is an unknown American heroine in her relentless pursuit of a national day of being thankful. This true story follows the thirty-eight years it took to secure Thanksgiving as a national holiday.

Musical Selection

Sound recording: track 9, "Table Grace." *Gratitude, Gravy & Garrison* by Vocal Essence Chorus. Orcas, WA: Clarion, 2010, compact disc.

Questions

Print the questions on a TURKEY shape (download pattern 3.10 at alaeditions/webextras) and laminate them. Have a plastic pumpkin to place the questions in as they rotate around your discussion circle.

- What is your favorite part of Thanksgiving?
- How would you feel if Thanksgiving was to be cancelled?
- Do you think Sarah's efforts were worthwhile? Why or why not?
- Why is Thanksgiving an important holiday?

- How does your family celebrate Thanksgiving?
- Is there anything you would think important enough to work toward for thirty-eight years?
- Did you know about Sarah before reading this book?
- Why is Sarah called a "superhero"?
- Have you ever sent a letter to someone to persuade them to do what you want? Who and for what?

Game: Pumpkin Race

- Break the class into two teams. Teams form a single-file line.
- Each team is given a small pumpkin and a yard stick.
- On the go signal, the racers use the stick to roll the pumpkins to the finish line.
- The first team to have all their players push the pumpkin over the finish line wins!

Craft: Straw Hat Turkey

- Glue five craft sticks behind the straw hat where you would like the back feathers.
- Use precut shapes of felt for the back feathers, beaks, wings, and wattle. Download pattern 3.11 at alaeditions.org/webextras.
- Glue the back feathers to the craft sticks. Allow glue from feathers to dry.
- Glue on the wings, eyes, wattle, and beak.
- Twist the stems into feet for the turkey and glue them on.

Materials

- discussion questions, cut and laminated
- audio CD and player
- 2 small pumpkins or gourds
- 2 yardsticks
- straw craft hats
- yellow, orange, red, and brown felt sheets
- feather pattern (1 per child)
- craft sticks (5 per child)
- orange chenille stems
- googly eyes
- craft glue

Fall, Week 6

Too Many Pumpkins

Book: Too Many Pumpkins

White, Linda. *Too Many Pumpkins*. New York: Holiday House, 1996.
- A giant pumpkin lands in Rebecca's yard, splattering seeds everywhere. What is a pumpkin hater to do when she is overrun with pumpkins?

Musical Selection

Sound recording: track 2, "Big Pumpkin." *Big Pumpkin* by Mr. Billy. WI: Doctors Orders Music, 2009, compact disc.

Questions

Print the questions on a PUMPKIN shape (download pattern 3.12 at alaeditions.org/webextras) and laminate them. Have a plastic pumpkin to place the questions in as they rotate around your discussion circle.
- What do you think Rebecca will do next Halloween?
- Are there any foods you really do not like?
- What are some other things you could do with pumpkins?
- Have you ever had a problem that kept getting worse? What was it?
- Who really came to visit Rebecca and the Jack-o'-lanterns?
- Does ignoring a problem ever make the problem go away? Why or why not?
- Do you think Rebecca still hates pumpkins? Why or why not?
- Have you ever been to a pumpkin patch?
- Do you think Rebecca will plant pumpkins again? Why or why not?
- Is it possible for pumpkins to grow as they did in the story?
- What would you have done to get rid of the pumpkins?
- Has your family ever eaten so much of one thing that you became sick of it? What was it?

Game: Pin the Face on the Pumpkin

Preparation: Draw and cut out a large pumpkin shape from orange poster board and tape it to the wall. Cut different shapes for eyes, noses, and mouths from black construction paper (download pattern 3.13 at alaeditions .org/webextras). Laminate the pieces and put tape on the backs. Lay the pieces on a tray.

- Children form a single-file line. Place a blindfold on the first player and have her choose a facial feature from the tray. Gently spin the child around two times and point her in the direction of the pumpkin face.
- The child sticks the eye, nose, or mouth onto the pumpkin.
- Each child selects a different facial part until a complete jack-o'-lantern is built. The pumpkins may look silly with three noses, six eyes, one mouth, and so on . . .
- Once a face is completed, remove the pieces and start again. Repeat the game as often as time allows.

Craft: Mini Pumpkins

- Cut two cups from a cardboard egg carton and glue one on top of the other, making sure the edges are in alignment.
- Once the glue dries, paint the shell with orange acrylic paint. If time is an issue, you can cut, glue, and paint beforehand.
- Poke a hole in the top with a paper clip.
- Make a stem and curly vines from green chenille stems and push the ends through the hole.
- Use a black permanent marker to draw on a jack-o'-lantern face.

Materials

- discussion questions, cut and laminated
- audio CD and player
- plastic jack-o'-lantern
- blindfold
- wall-size pumpkin and laminated facial features
- tape
- cardboard egg cartons (not plastic or Styrofoam)
- glue
- orange acrylic paint
- black permanent markers
- green chenille stems
- paper clip

Winter, Week 1

Moi and Marie Antoinette

Book: Moi and Marie Antoinette

Cullen, Lynn. *Moi and Marie Antoinette*. New York: Bloomsbury Children's Books: Distributed to the trade by Holtzbrinck Publishers, 2006.

- Sebastian, the devoted pet to young Marie Antoinette, tells about Marie's life from age 13 through her coronation as the French queen and into motherhood. The pug provides a whimsical look into the unhappy life of the eighteenth-century royal.

Musical Selection

French Music for Horn & Piano by Guglielmo Pellarin. Detmold, Germany: Audite, 2011, compact disc.

Questions

Print the questions on a TIARA shape (download pattern 3.14 at alaeditions.org/webextras) and laminate them. Have a fancy hat to place the questions in as they rotate around your discussion circle.

- Why was Sebastian unhappy when Antoinette had the baby?
- Why was it important for Antoinette to get married?
- Do you think Therese was happy as an adult?
- Would you like being dressed by strangers or watched as you ate dinner? Why or why not?
- What would be a perfect life for Sebastian?
- Why do you think Sebastian and Therese become friends?
- What do you think about being asked to marry someone you never met?
- How do you think Antoinette felt as she left for France?
- Why was Sebastian finally happy?
- Was Therese like her mother? How?
- Why do you think Antoinette didn't play with Sebastian in France?
- How might the story be different if it was told by Antoinette?

Game: Belle of the Ball Costume Game

- Divide the children into two teams for a relay.
- Set out two boxes of costume jewelry, tiaras, and high heels. (Have an equal amount in each box.)
- The groups form two straight lines. Each player in turn puts on all the articles in the box, takes them all off, and returns it to the box. The finished player passes the box to a teammate and sits down.
- The first group to have every child put on and take off all the accessories and sit down in a straight line wins!

Craft: Dog Bone Dog

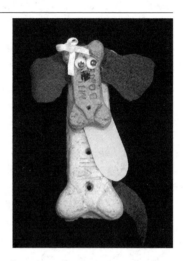

- Use the patterns and precut a set of ears from brown felt, a tongue from pink felt, and a nose from black felt. (Download pattern 3.15 at alaeditions.org/webextras.)
- Glue the ears and tongue onto the smaller dog bone. Glue the tail onto the larger bone. Add the googly eyes and bow.
- Glue the small bone onto the large bone.
- Optional: glue a magnet on the back of the large bone.

Materials

- discussion questions, cut and laminated
- audio CD and player
- fancy hat
- 2 copy paper boxes of dress-up clothes and accessories
  Optional: Wrap the outside of the boxes with fancy princess wrapping paper.
- small dog treats
- large dog treats
- googly eyes
- ribbon
- black felt
- brown felt
- pink felt
- craft glue
- magnets (optional)

Winter, Week 2

No Roses for Harry

Book: No Roses for Harry

Zion, Gene. *No Roses for Harry.* New York: Harper, 1958.

  - Harry (the Dirty Dog) is not impressed with the gifts he receives from his grandmother. The latest silly green sweater with yellow roses is the worst. Harry does all he can to be rid of the hated present.

Musical Selection

Sound recording: track 1, "Maxwell, the Dancing Dog." *Maxwell, the Dancing Dog: Songs for Children of All Ages* by Jeff Moyer. Cleveland Heights, OH: Music from the Heart, 2001, compact disc.

Questions

Print the questions on a SWEATER shape (download pattern 3.16 at alaeditions.org/webextras) and laminate them. Have an old sewing box to place the questions in as they rotate around your discussion circle.

  - Have you ever received a gift you didn't like? What did you do?
  - Why do people give gifts?
  - What should you do if you don't like a gift?
  - Have you ever tried to lose something on purpose? If so, what was it?
  - How would you feel if someone didn't like a gift you made them?
  - How do you think Harry felt when everyone laughed at him?
  - How do you think the family felt before Grandma came to visit?
  - Should Harry have stopped the bird from taking the sweater?
  - Should dogs wear sweaters? Why or why not?
  - Was losing the sweater a good plan? What else could Harry have done?
  - How do you think Grandma felt when she saw the bird nest?
  - How do you show people that you are thankful for their gifts?

Game: Sweater Race

- Divide the children into two teams for a relay. Have the teams form straight lines.
- Give each team a button-down sweater. Each child puts on the sweater, buttons it up, unbuttons it, takes it off, and passes it to the next teammate. After that teammate has the sweater, the first child may sit down.
- The first team to complete the challenge and have all members sitting in a straight line wins.

Craft: Paper Bag Bird Nest

- Cut off the top three-quarters of a brown paper lunch bag.
- Scrunch the bottom of the bag down a bit.
- Fill the bottom of the bag with green Easter grass.
- Use the top three-quarters of the bag to cut horizontal circular strips. (Cut horizontally across the lunch bag, leaving the strips intact.)
- Slide on, arrange, and glue the circular strips haphazardly around the outside of the nest to look like twigs.

Materials

- discussion questions, cut and laminated
- audio CD and player
- basket
- 2 old button-down sweaters
- brown paper lunch bags
- scissors
- green Easter grass or thinly cut green streamers
- craft glue

Winter, Week 3

The Princess and the Pizza

Book: The Princess and the Pizza

Auch, Mary Jane. *The Princess and the Pizza.* New York: Holiday House, 2002.
- In a twist on the princess and the pea story, Princess Paulina must compete for the hand of Prince Drupert. She passes the traditional pea test and the glass-slipper fitting, but struggles in the third trial: she must use flour, yeast, water, tomatoes, and cheese to create a tempting feast.

Musical Selection

Sound recording: track 1, "That's Amore." *That's Amore: Italian-American Favorites.* Los Angeles, CA: Shout Factory, 2008, compact disc.

Questions

Print the questions on a PIZZA shape (download pattern 3.17 at alaeditions.org/webextras) and laminate them. Have a clean pizza box to place the questions in as they rotate around your discussion circle.

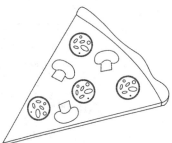

- Have you ever heard of a story similar to this one? What was it?
- What might Pauline have written in her essay about Queen Zelda?
- What do you think Pauline did after she left the castle?
- Do you think the princess test was fair? Why or why not?
- Why do you think Pauline wouldn't share her pizza recipe with the queen?
- Who are some of the other princesses in the book?
- What other names could Pauline have given her dish?
- What does Pauline mean when she says, "That is so once upon a time?"
- Do you think Queen Zelda and Pauline's father would be a good match? Why or why not?

- What kind of jobs could a princess get?
- Does your family have any secret recipes? If so, for what?
- Do you know of any other foods or recipes that were created by mistake?
- Why do you think Queen Zelda wouldn't help Pauline get her fair share of the ingredients?
- Would you like being a prince or princess? Why or why not?
- Do queens have to be fair? Why or why not?

Game: Pizza Dice Throw

- Pass out the direction sheets, game boards (download patterns 3.18 a and b at alaeditions.org/webextras), crayons, and dice.
- Divide children into groups of two, three, or four. Be sure one child in each group can read the directions.
- The first child in each group to finish coloring their pizza wins!

Craft: Paper Pizza

- Give each child a paper plate and a large circle of tan or brown construction paper.
- Glue the circle onto the plate to make the pizza crust.
- (Use your scrap box if you have one.) Children cut and glue small red paper circles (pepperoni), scraps of yellow (cheese), green (peppers), white (mushrooms), black (olives), and so on onto the brown circle crust to create their own pizza.

Materials

- discussion questions, cut and laminated
- audio CD and player
- clean pizza box
- game directions
- dice (1 per group)
- game boards (1 per child)
- crayons
- paper plates
- circles of brown or tan construction paper
- glue
- construction paper scraps

Winter, Week 4

Rocks in His Head

Book: Rocks in His Head

Hurst, Carol Otis. *Rocks in His Head.* New York: Greenwillow Books, 2001.
- The author tells the story of her father, who was an avid rock collector throughout his life. During the Depression he is forced to work as a janitor in the science museum. It is there that his passion for rocks draws him some attention.

Musical Selection

Sound recording: track 1, "Brother, Can You Spare a Dime?" *The Great Depression: American Music in the 30's.* New York: Columbia, 1993, compact disc.

Questions

Print the questions on a POCKET shape (download pattern 3.19 at alaeditions.org/webextras) and laminate them. Have a basket to place the questions in as they rotate around your discussion circle.

- What do you think it means to have "rocks in your pocket and rocks in your head"?
- Is it important that a hobby can make you money? Why or why not?
- Is a college education important? Why or why not?
- Do you have a collection? If so, of what?
- What would it be like to not have a car?
- Have you ever lived through "tough times"?
- Do you think the father had rocks in his head? Why or why not?
- Do you carry anything in your pocket all the time? What? Why?
- Why do you think the father accepted the job as a janitor?
- Would you stop at a gas station to look through a rock collection? Why or why not?
- What is interesting about rocks?
- Is there anything you would like about living during this time period?
- What would you dislike about living during this time period?

- Have you ever heard anyone say, "You have rocks in your head?"
- Can you think of any other expressions for someone who is always thinking about a particular hobby?
- Have you ever seen a rock collection before? Where?

Game: Idiom Charades

- Explain that an *idiom* is a phrase where the meaning is not literal. Give several examples, such as "kick the bucket," "eat your words," and so on.
- Cut out and laminate the idiom cards (download pattern 3.20 at alaeditions.org/webextras).
- Play charades with the idioms. The child acting looks at the card, and the rest of the group guesses what the phrase may be.
- Optional: With younger groups, list and discuss a "phrase bank" on the blackboard to help the children with their guessing.

Craft: Poetry Pebbles

- Gather about twenty-five small pebbles or rocks per child. Be sure they are clean and dry.
- Use fine-tip permanent markers to write words onto your pebbles. Choose different sorts of words—people, places, things, action words—and some punctuation marks. For example: he/she/to/love/ dog/went/walk/you/happy/in/sweet/a/my/your/blue/red/purple/ pretty/flower/./!/?
- Let the marker dry and then spray the pebbles with hairspray to seal.
- Roll your pebble set to start a poem or story.
- Place each pebble set into a bag for each child to take home.

Materials

- discussion questions, cut and laminated
- audio CD and player
- basket
- idiom (charade) cards, cut and laminated
- pebbles (25 or 30 per child)
- fine-tip permanent markers
- plastic bags to hold pebble sets (1 per child)
- hairspray

Winter, Week 5

Snowflake Bentley

Book: Snowflake Bentley

Martin, Jacqueline Briggs. *Snowflake Bentley.* Boston: Houghton Mifflin, 1998.
- The reader learns of the life of Wilson Bentley, a real person, told as a fictional story. His curiosity about snowflakes and passion for photography lead to two discoveries. Willie discovers that no two snowflakes are alike, and each one is startlingly beautiful.

Musical Selection

Sound recording: disk 2, track 18, "Waltz of the Snowflake." *Simply Christmas.* London: Decca Music Group, 2003, compact disc.

Questions

Print the questions on a SNOWFLAKE shape (download pattern 3.21 at alaeditions.org/webextras) and laminate them. Have a knit cap to place the questions in as they rotate around your discussion circle.

- Are you interested in anything your parents call foolish? What?
- Why do you think Willie was so interested in snow?
- How do you think Willie felt when his neighbors didn't want to look at his photographs?
- How else could Willie save snow crystals?
- What is your favorite thing about snow?
- Why do you think Willie did not give up trying to take a picture of a snowflake?
- Do you think Willie's work with photographing snow was important? Why or why not?
- Do you have any hobbies that could become a career? What?
- Do you have any collections? Of what?
- If you could start a collection of photographs, what would the photos be of?

- Are there any jobs with snow that could make a person rich?
- What is ironic about the way Snowflake Bentley died?

Game: Sled Pull Relay Race

- Divide the group into two teams. The children form two single-file lines. Draw a chalk finish line about fifteen to twenty feet away from the two teams.
- The first child pulls a child behind him on a plastic sled to the finish line. The riding child runs back to the line and pulls the next child, and so on until all children have been pulled across the finish line. When they have taken a ride, they return to their team's line and sit down.
- The team that has all their members sitting in a single file line after the finish line (and after all children have pulled and been pulled) wins!

Craft: Pasta Wheel Snowflake

- Give each child an 8½-by-11-inch piece of waxed paper.
- Use a large amount of glue to stick uncooked, wheel-shaped pasta noodles in a snowflake pattern on the wax paper. The wheels must touch one another.
- Sprinkle silver glitter over the noodles before the glue has dried.
- Let dry on the waxed paper (perhaps even until next week).
- When the glue is completely dry and transparent, remove the waxed paper gently.
- Tie a thin string of thread to the uppermost noodle to create an ornament.
- Optional: Spray with hairspray to preserve. Place in plastic bag for transportation home.

Materials

- discussion questions, cut and laminated
- audio CD and player
- knit hat
- 2 plastic sleds with rope or handles for pulling
- waxed paper
- pasta wheels
- school glue
- silver glitter
- white thread

Winter, Week 6

Strega Nona: An Old Tale

Book: Strega Nona: An Old Tale

DePaola, Tommie. *Strega Nona: An Old Tale*. Englewood Cliffs, NJ: Prentice Hall, 1975.

 - Strega Nona is the most helpful villager in her Italian neighborhood. She helps her friends with all their troubles. Unbeknown to them, she is assisted by her magic pasta pot. When she leaves town and leaves her hired hand alone with the pot, trouble boils over!

Musical Selection

Sound recording: track 1, "That's Amore." *That's Amore: Italian-American Favorites*. Los Angeles, CA: Shout Factory, 2008, compact disc.

Questions

Print the questions on a POT shape (download pattern 3.22 at alaeditions.org/webextras) and laminate them. Have a cooking pot to place the questions in as they rotate around your discussion circle.

 - Why do you think Big Anthony disobeyed Strega Nona?
 - Why do you think Big Anthony was angry when the townspeople laughed at him?
 - What are some ways Big Anthony could prove he was not lying about the pasta pot?
 - Do you think Big Anthony will make the same mistake again? Why or why not?
 - Why does Big Anthony want to show the townspeople the pasta pot?
 - What does "the punishment must fit the crime" mean?
 - What do you think caused Big Anthony's problem?
 - What is Big Anthony's responsibility to Strega Nona?
 - How would you have punished Big Anthony?
 - What does Big Anthony do that is NOT responsible?

- Do you think Strega Nona will leave Big Anthony alone with the pasta pot again?
- Have you ever had the responsibility of caring for another person's possessions? How did you do?
- Have you ever been NOT paying attention and missed an important part of directions? What happened?
- Do you believe in magic? Why or why not?
- How does Strega Nona show she cares about the people of Calabria?

Game: Learn a Magic Trick: The Jumping Rubber Band

Find directions and illustrations here: www.goodtricks.net/band.html.

Craft: My Own Magic Pot

- Print out one empty pot per child (download pattern 3.23 at alaeditions.org/webextras).
- Ask, "If you could have a pot like Strega Nona's, what would you like it to produce?" Examples: ice cream, candy, fruit.
- Instruct the children to cut out pictures of the food they wish for out of old magazines and to glue their pictures onto their pot. They may choose to color and fill in the pot using markers.

Materials

- discussion questions, cut and laminated
- audio CD and player
- pot
- rubber bands
- Magic Pot template
- scissors
- magazines
- glue
- markers

Spring, Week 1

Letters from a Desperate Dog

Book: Letters from a Desperate Dog

Madison, Alan. *Letters from a Desperate Dog.* New York: Schwartz & Wade Books, 2007.

> - Emma the pup can never please her master. In her frustration she writes to the newspaper advice column. She is advised to leave home and search for a place where she will be appreciated. She takes the advice but can't seem to stop thinking about her master.

Musical Selection

Sound recording: track 2, "I Love My Dog." *Disney's 101 Dalmations and Friends.* Burbank, CA: Walt Disney Records, 2008, compact disc .

Questions

Print the questions on a BONE shape (download pattern 3.24 at alaeditions.org/webextras) and laminate them. Have a dog bowl to place the questions in as they rotate around your discussion circle.

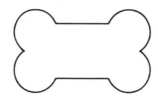

- Is George a good pet owner? Why or why not?
- Who do you ask for advice?
- What do you think Emma learned from her adventures?
- What problems (if any) do you have with your pet?
- If your pet could complain, what would it complain about?
- Have you ever needed advice about a dilemma? What was the dilemma?
- Why are the "MISSING" posters so important to George?
- Do you think Queenie gives good advice? Why or why not?
- Do you think this story ended "happy ever after"?
- Can you think of a time you were trying to be helpful but you got in trouble instead?

- What does it mean to be unreasonable?
- Why do you think there is a cat in the story?
- Do you think Emma was a good dog or a bad dog? Why?
- What are some other problems dog owners could have?
- How else could Emma have solved her problems with George?
- What problems could dogs have with their owners?

Game: Doggie, Doggie, Where's Your Bone?

- Choose a child to be the doggie. He should cover his eyes, wear a blindfold, or step out of the room for a moment.
- The remaining children sit in a circle on the floor. Give another child a rawhide bone to hide in her hands. Once the bone is hidden, call back the doggie. All the children hide their hands behind their backs and chant:

> Doggie, doggie where's your bone?
> Somebody stole it from your home.
> Guess who! Maybe you!

- The doggie has three guesses to find who is hiding his bone.
- If the doggie is right, the person holding the bone becomes doggie. If he is wrong, he is the doggie again, and the bone is given to a different child to hide.

Craft: Dashing Dog Envelope

- Use the templates (download pattern 3.25 at alaeditions.org/webextras) or allow the children to create their own dog parts.
- The children cut out and color ears, a tail, a nose, and paws.
- Fold in the corners of the envelope for the ears. Glue the parts onto the envelope to create a dog.
- Let glue dry and decorate further with crayons or markers.

Materials

- discussion questions, cut and laminated
- audio CD and player
- dog bowl
- rawhide bone
- white envelopes
- colored construction paper
- markers or crayons

- scissors
- glue
- dog envelope patterns

Spring, Week 2

My Great-Aunt Arizona

Book: My Great-Aunt Arizona

Houston, Gloria. *My Great-Aunt Arizona*. New York: HarperCollins, 1992.
- Growing up in a log cabin, Arizona dreamed of traveling and seeing the world. While she never leaves her one-room schoolhouse, she teaches students that they have their own ability to read and dream of the faraway places she would never visit.

Musical Selection

Sound recording: track 5, "Old Log Cabin." *Deep in the Mountains* by Longview. Burlington, MA: Rounder Records, 2008, compact disc.

Questions

Print the questions on an APPLE shape (download pattern 3.1 at alaeditions.org/webextras) and laminate them. Have an apple basket to place the questions in as they rotate around your discussion circle.

- What has stayed the same about schools? What is different?
- How would your life be different if you lived in a log cabin?
- What could be another name for a "blab" school?
- Do you know why you were given your name? Why?
- Where do you dream of going? Why?
- Do you know any teachers like Arizona? Who?
- What makes a teacher "good"?
- Would you like to have Arizona as a teacher? Why or why not?
- Would you like to have all grades of students in your classroom?
- What would be good for teachers in a one-room schoolhouse?
- Do you think Arizona's students went to "faraway places"? Why or why not?

- What about teaching in a one-room schoolhouse would be bad for teachers?

Game: William Matrimmatoe

Explain to the children that games were simpler in the days of Arizona. They often were handed down from generation to generation and received the name of a family. This is an example. It is played like Duck, Duck, Goose.

- All children sit in a circle except one, who is left standing.
- The standing child walks around the circle tapping each head as she chants:

> William Matrimmatoe,
> He's a good fisherman.
> He catches hens,
> Puts them in pens.
> Some lay eggs,
> Some lay none.
> William Matrimmatoe,
> He's a good fisherman.
> Wire, briar, lumber, lock,
> Three geese in a flock.
> One flew east,
> One flew west,
> One flew over the cuckoo's nest.
> Wire, briar, lumber, lock,
> Out goes YOU.

- The player whose head is tapped on *YOU* stands up and chases the tapper. The child who sits down is "safe," and the child left standing is the tapper for the next round. Help the children with the chant. Write it in the story room so confident readers can read it.

Craft: Yarn Dolls

- Wrap the yarn twenty to thirty times around the piece of cardboard the long way. Then take a short piece of yarn and slip it under the wrapped yarn.
- Pull the short piece of yarn to the top of the cardboard. Tie all the yarn together tightly with a double knot.

- Cut off the ends of the short piece of yarn close to the knot. Then cut the yarn open at the bottom of the cardboard.
- Place the yarn over the ball. Arrange the yarn so it covers the ball completely.
- Use another piece of yarn to tie the yarn together at the bottom of the ball.
- Cut off the ends of the short piece of yarn close to the knot.
- Make the dolls body and arms; divide the rest of the yarn into four equal sections.
- Use two short pieces of yarn to tie the outer sections of yarn halfway down. Cut off the ends of the short pieces of yarn close to the knots.
- Tie the two middle sections together about a third of the way down with a short piece of yarn. Cut off the ends close to the knot.
- Make the dolls legs by dividing the remaining yarn into two equal sections.
- Tie each leg with a short piece of yarn. Cut off close to knot.
- Glue on buttons for eyes and ribbon for nose and mouth. If you like, make small bows to place in each doll's hair. Scrap yarn is useful for creating hair.
- Some may wish to braid the legs and arms before tying off.

Materials

- discussion questions, cut and laminated
- audio CD and player
- basket
- yarn (12 yards per child)
- 5-inch pieces of yarn (7 per child)
- 7-by-5-inch pieces of cardboard (1 per child)
- scissors
- Styrofoam balls, 1 inch in diameter (1 per child)
- fabric glue
- 1/4 -inch buttons
- bits of ribbon and yarn for hair, bows, a nose, and a mouth

Spring, Week 3

Nora's Ark

Title: Nora's Ark

Kinsey-Warnock, Natalie. *Nora's Ark*. New York: HarperCollins, 2005.
  - Grandpa is building a new house on a hill, but Grandma is not thrilled to leave the home where she raised her children. During the Vermont Flood of 1927, the new house on the hill saves not only the family but twenty-three neighbors, three horses, a cow, five pigs, a duck, four cats, and a hundred chickens.

Musical Selection

Sound recording: track 15, "The Storm." *25 Thunderous Favorites*. Hauppauge, NY: SPJ Music, 2000, compact disc.

Questions

Print the questions on an ARK shape (download pattern 3.26 at alaeditions.org/webextras) and laminate them. Have a basket to place the questions in as they rotate around your discussion circle.

- What did Grandma mean when she said, "That house is just gravy"?
- Have you ever faced a dangerous situation? What was it?
- What are some things that are "just gravy?"
- Why do you think Grandma wanted to stay in her old house?
- Why do you think Grandpa let the cows and horses out of the barn?
- Does this story remind you of any other stories you may have heard? Were those stories true or make-believe?
- What might you say if you saw a cow in a tree?
- What do you think the people in the new house were thinking about as it rained?
- Who do you think worried the most? Why?
- Who were the heroes of the story? Why?
- What are some things that are "potatoes"?

Game: Nora's Ark Dice Game

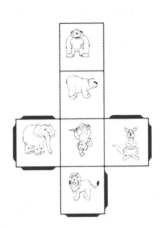

- Pass out the direction sheets, game boards (download patterns 3.27 a, b, and c at alaeditions.org/webextras), scissors, glue, and dice pattern.
- Divide children into groups of two, three, or four. Be sure one child in each group can read the directions.
- Children cut out, fold, and tape their die together.
- The first child in each group with all six animals in their ark wins!

Craft: Animal Cracker Ark

- Give each child an ark pattern (download pattern 3.28 at alaeditions.org/webextras) for them to color and cut out.
- Tape together two pieces of blue construction paper to make one large piece of blue.
- Dip a toothpick into blue paint and paint raindrops on the blue construction paper.
- Let paint dry.
- Glue the ark onto the blue construction paper.
- Glue on cotton ball clouds.
- Glue additional animal crackers onto the ark.

Materials

- discussion questions, cut and laminated
- audio CD and player
- basket
- dice (1 per group)
- game instructions (1 per group)
- ark game board (one per child)
- scissors
- glue
- ark pattern (1 per child)
- blue construction paper
- blue paint
- toothpicks
- cotton balls
- Nabisco Barnum's Animal Crackers (plain)

Important: Recognizing that the health and safety of children is of the utmost importance, the foods listed in this resource are free of the most common four food allergens: eggs, peanuts, tree nuts, and milk. Deviating from the brand name will not assure allergen safety. For more information, see http://snack safely.com/snackguide

Spring, Week 4

Piggie Pie

Book: Piggie Pie

Palatini, Margie. *Piggie Pie!* New York: Clarion Books, 1995.

- When Gritch the Witch gets a craving for Piggie Pie, she heads to Old MacDonald's farm in search of piggies. When she arrives, there are no pigs to be found. Where have all those piggies gone?

Musical Selection

Sound recording: track 3, "Old MacDonald Had a Farm." *Singin' & Groovin': 25 Best Sing-along Songs.* Redway, CA: Music for Little People. Distributed by Los Angeles, CA: Rhino Records, 2010, compact disc.

Questions

Print the questions on a PIG shape (download pattern 3.29 at alaeditions.org/webextras) and laminate them. Have a witch hat to place the questions in as they rotate around your discussion circle.

- Why weren't the piggies afraid of Gritch?
- Was there anything strange about the farm?
- Gritch called the pigs "porkers" and "piggies." What are other names for pigs?
- Where else might Gritch have found pigs?
- What other stories were hinted at?
- Why might older people find the book funny when preschoolers do not?
- If you were making a pie for a witch, what would you put in it?
- When you wake up hungry, what do you have a taste for?
- Who else might enjoy eating "Piggie Pie"?
- Where do you think the pigs kept their costumes?
- How else could the pigs have escaped Gritch?
- What do you think happened when the wolf and Gritch went to lunch?

Game: Hot Piggy

Play like hot potato, but instead of passing around a potato, use a stuffed pig.
- Children sit on floor in a circle.
- Play music. While the music is playing, the children pass around a stuffed animal pig. When the music stops, the child holding the pig is "out."
- The last child in the circle wins!
- Repeat the game several times.

Craft: Broom Pencils

- Cut several two-inch strips of raffia per child.
- Tape the raffia to the eraser end of the pencil to make a broom.
- Take a short piece of chenille stem and twist it around the top of the raffia to cover the tape.

Materials

- discussion questions, cut and laminated
- audio CD and player
- witch hat
- stuffed pig
- yellow pencils
- raffia
- white chenille stem
- tape

Spring, Week 5

Rainbow Fish

Book: Rainbow Fish

Pfister, Marcus. *The Rainbow Fish*. New York: North-South Books, 1992.
- Rainbow Fish, with his glittery scales, is the most admired and beautiful creature in the ocean. But his pride alienates all the other sea life. The octopus advises Rainbow Fish to boast less and be generous with his special scales. Eventually Rainbow Fish discovers that giving away his beauty helps him earn friends and happiness.

Musical Selection

Sound recording: track 1, "Come Swim with Me." *The Rainbow Fish: Come Swim with Me.* Del Mar, CA: Genius Entertainment, 2003, compact disc.

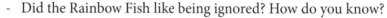

Questions

Print the questions on a FISH shape (download pattern 3.30 at alaeditions.org/webextras) and laminate them. Have a goldfish bowl to place the questions in as they rotate around your discussion circle.

- Did the octopus give good advice? Why?
- Would you give something away to gain a friend? Why?
- Did the Rainbow Fish like being ignored? How do you know?
- Why do you think the Rainbow Fish wanted nothing to do with the other fish?
- How do you feel when you share?
- What things do you have that are easy to share? How about hard to share?
- Do you know anyone who doesn't try to get along with the group?
- What would you do if you knew some people didn't want you around? How would you feel?
- How do you think the Rainbow Fish felt after giving away his scales?
- Why did the Rainbow Fish think he was special? Do you think he was special?
- Do you have something that makes you special, like the Rainbow Fish's scale? What?
- How did the octopus help Rainbow Fish?

Game

Divide children into groups of three or four and play the card game "Chomp" or "Go Fish."

Craft: Rainbow Fish

- The children cut out the fish pattern.
- Decorate fish with bingo dabbers, markers, and circle sequins.

Materials

- discussion questions, cut and laminated
- audio CD and player
- goldfish bowl
- fish pattern
- scissors
- glue
- bingo dabbers
- sequins
- markers
- Chomp game or Go Fish cards

Spring, Week 6

Teammates

Book: Teammates

Barber, Tiki. *Teammates.* New York: Simon & Schuster Books for Young Readers, 2006.

- NFL players and identical twins Tiki and Ronde Barber share one of their childhood memories. Tiki fumbles the football in a preseason practice game, and his teammates question his talent. With help from a coach and a lot of practice, the brothers learn together that practice makes perfect.

Musical Selection

Sound recording: track 16, "Huddle, Huddle, Huddle Along (The Football Song)" by The Wiggles. *Racing to the Rainbow.* New York: Koch Records, 2007, compact disc.

Questions

Print the questions on a FOOTBALL shape (download pattern 3.31 at alaeditions.org/webextras) and laminate them. Have a popcorn tub to place the questions in as they rotate around your discussion circle.

- Do only good football players need confidence?
- Other than football, what are some things you need to practice in order to get better?
- Do your brothers and sisters teach you anything? What?
- Would your feelings about the story change if the Vikings lost their final football game?
- Paco called Tiki "Velcro." Can you think of any other nicknames for him?
- How do you think Ronde felt when he had to tell his brother that the team didn't want him to carry the ball as much? How about Tiki?
- Does practice REALLY always make perfect?
- Do you think all mistakes are supposed to happen?
- What does it take to be a good teammate?
- What do you wish your brothers or sisters would teach you?
- How did Tiki and Ronde's team help them?
- What are some things you find yourself to be good at?

Game: Paper Football

The object of the game is to score touchdowns.

- Have the children choose a partner. High score wins. (Younger children may just want to count touchdowns as one point as opposed to the typical six.)
- Play on a straight-edged table with opponents sitting across from each other. Players take turns.
- To get a touchdown, a player must flick the ball with her finger and have the ball stop, with part of it sticking over the table.
- After a touchdown, the player kicks an extra point. Whoever is kicking holds the ball vertically between his fingers and the table. With his other hand he flicks the ball with his finger. The other player holds a goal post by placing her thumbs together and using her index fingers as the goal posts.

To make the football:
- Fold an 8½-by-11-inch piece of paper in half to make one long skinny piece.
- Cut or tear along the seam.
- Holding the paper so it's long, fold the corner down into a triangle.
- Continue to fold down, making triangles until you run out of paper to fold.
- Tuck any excess paper into the "pocket" on the top of the ball.

Craft: Stuffed Football

- On a flat brown grocery bag, draw a football shape. Cut through both layers so you have two identical football shapes. Set the scraps aside.
- Crinkle your two football shapes. Put them in a tub of water for a minute.
- Let the paper dry flat. Don't press out all the wrinkles, you want a leather effect.
- Use a hole punch to punch two parallel rows of six holes.
- Use six pieces of white yarn to string through the holes.
- Staple your football shapes together along the edges. Leave a four-to-five-inch opening.
- Stuff your football with the leftover paper bag scraps, torn and crumbled into little pieces. If necessary, add additional scrap paper.
- Close the opening with staples.

Materials

- discussion questions, cut and laminated
- audio CD and player
- popcorn tub
- paper to make paper footballs
- brown grocery bags (1 per child)
- scissors
- white yarn
- tape
- tub of water
- stapler and staples
- scrap paper

Summer, Week 1

Lyle, Lyle, Crocodile

Book: Lyle, Lyle, Crocodile

Waber, Bernard. *Lyle, Lyle, Crocodile*. Boston, MA: Houghton Mifflin, 1965.
  - Lyle the crocodile is happy living in his apartment with the Primms
    on 88th Street in New York. A cranky neighbor puts Lyle in the zoo but
    experiences a change of heart when the crocodile saves him from a fire.

Musical Selection

Sound recording: track 3, "Never Smile at a Crocodile." *Animal Rock.* Burbank,
CA: Disney/Walt Disney Records, 2001, compact disc.

Questions

Print the questions on a CROCODILE shape (download pattern 3.32 at alaeditions.org/webextras) and
laminate them. Have a basket to place the questions
in as they rotate around your discussion circle.

- Do you think Lyle belongs in the zoo? Why?
- What words would you use to describe Lyle?
- Why do you think Mr. Grumps forgave Lyle?
- How is Lyle like a human?
- What words would you use to describe Mr. Grumps?
- What would you do if a crocodile was smiling at you?
- How is Lyle different from real crocodiles?
- Can Lyle be TOO friendly? Why?
- What would you do if Lyle was scaring your cat?
- Would you like a crocodile for a pet? Why or why not?
- How would a real crocodile adjust to live in New York City?
- What was Mr. Grump's mistake about Lyle?

Game: Crocodile Egg Hunt

- Before your club meets, hide twenty to thirty large plastic eggs in a
  small outside area. Check your library's policy on taking a group out-
  doors. If necessary, hide the eggs in your story room.

- Discuss with the children how crocodiles hide their eggs in the sand to protect them from predators.
- Take the children to the area where the eggs are hidden and let the hunt begin! If you choose, you can place stickers or some other small treat in each egg.
- The children race to collect the eggs. The one who collects the most wins!

Craft: Clothespin Crocodile

- Paint a wooden clothespin green. Allow to dry.
- When dry, add googly eyes and white craft foam teeth to create a crocodile.

Materials

- discussion questions, cut and laminated
- audio CD and player
- 30 large plastic Easter eggs
- wooden clothespins
- green tempera paint
- paintbrushes
- glue
- googly eyes
- scissors
- white craft foam

Summer, Week 2

Players in Pigtails

Book: Players in Pigtails

Corey, Shana. *Players in Pigtails*. New York: Scholastic Press, 2003.
- Katie Casey, a fictional character, helps start the All-American Girls Professional Baseball League. The AAGPBL is a real league that gave women the opportunity to play professional baseball while American men were involved in World War II.

Musical Selection

Sound recording: track 1, "Take Me Out to the Ball Game." *A Century of Baseball in Song* by Rick Miller. United States: Cape Song, 2005, compact disc.

Questions

Print the questions on a BASEBALL shape (download pattern 3.33 at alaeditions.org/webextras) and laminate them. Have a popcorn tub to place the questions in as they rotate around your discussion circle.

- How do you think the players felt when the fans laughed at them on Opening Day?
- What are some things that are considered to be "girl" things?
- Do you think some sports are only for boys and others only for girls? Why or why not?
- Did you know about the AAGPBL before reading this book?
- Why was it important for the players to look ladylike?
- What do most people think girls SHOULD like to do?
- Are there any sports that girls should never be allowed to play? Why or why not?
- Why don't professional baseball teams include girls now?
- Why do you think Katie's heart wasn't into cooking?
- Would you pay to go to a [insert local MLB team]'s game if girls were playing? Why or why not?
- What words would you use to describe Katie Casey?
- Why did the president want to keep baseball alive while the war was going on?
- How do you think Katie felt when she didn't make the high school baseball team?

Game

- Draw several bull's-eye targets on the walls around your story room.
- Give each child a Styrofoam ball and have them practice pitching at and aiming at the center of the bull's-eye.

Craft: Beaded Baseball Safety Pin

- Download pattern 3.34 at alaeditions.org/webextras.
- Open a safety pin and slip the seed beads onto it following the pattern: Each number column represents a pin; for example, your first pin will

have ten green beads. Your second pin will have three green beads, four white beads, and then three more green beads. The third pin will have two green, one red, four white, one more red, and then two more green beads. Continue following the pattern for pins 4 through 14.

- When you thread these beaded pins onto your large pin, start with the first pin.
- Put all the beaded pins onto a larger safety pin in order from 1 to 13. Slip the loop of the first beaded safety pin onto the large one.
- Once all thirteen beaded safety pins are in place and in order on the large safety pin, close it and you will have created a baseball.
- You may want to use pliers to squeeze the pin tight, assuring it stays closed.

Materials

- discussion questions, cut and laminated
- audio CD and player
- 8 Styrofoam balls, approximately 9 by 9 inches
- $\frac{1}{16}$-inch safety pins (13 per child)
- 2-inch safety pins (1 per child)
- green, red, and white seed beads
- pliers

Summer, Week 3

Velma Gratch & the Way Cool Butterfly

Book: Velma Gratch & the Way Cool Butterfly

Madison, Alan. *Velma Gratch & the Way Cool Butterfly*. New York: Schwartz & Wade Books, 2007.

- Velma Gratch feels lost in the shadows of her two older sisters. At first she misbehaves to get the attention of her first-grade class. But on a class trip to a butterfly conservatory, a monarch lands on Velma's finger and stays put—for days. Velma becomes popular with the help of her butterfly.

Musical Selection

Track 2: "Caterpillar Butterfly." *Caterpillar Butterfly: Songs to Help Kids Grow Wings* by David Grover. West Stockbridge, MA: National Children's Music Project, 2005, compact disc.

Questions

Print the questions on a BUTTERFLY shape (download pattern 3.35 at alaeditions.org/webextras) and laminate them. Have a butterfly net to place the questions in as they rotate around your discussion circle.

- Is it better to be the oldest or youngest child in the family? Why?
- What do you think teachers notice the most about you?
- Have you ever visited a butterfly conservatory? What was it like?
- Why do you think the butterfly was attracted to Velma?
- Are there any specific words you like to say? What are they?
- Could this story actually happen? Why or why not?
- How do you think Velma was feeling when the butterflies were landing on her classmates?
- Has your family ever acted like the monarch butterfly? Where did you fly?
- How do you think Velma felt on the first day of school?
- Why do you think the butterfly stayed so long on Velma's finger?
- What has been your favorite field trip?
- How did you feel on your first day of first grade?
- How could Velma have gotten the butterfly to leave?

Game: Chrysalis Game

- Pair each child with a partner.
- Children race as they wrap their partner in toilet paper as though it's a cocoon. The winner is the first pair who uses "wings" (their arms) to tear through the toilet paper chrysalis.
- Change who is being wrapped and repeat the race.

Craft: Baggie Butterfly

- Fill a baggie with scraps of colored tissue paper and colored cellophane that the children have ripped into small pieces. Tape the baggies closed with clear tape.
- Gather the baggie in the middle with a half of a chenille stem.
- Twist and bend the ends of the stem to form antennae.

Materials

- discussion questions, cut and laminated
- audio CD and player
- butterfly net
- rolls of toilet paper (1 per child)
- sandwich-size baggies
- scissors
- tissue paper
- colored cellophane
- green chenille stems
- tape

NOTE

1. Howard Gardner, *Frames of Mind: The Theory of Multiple Intelligences* (New York: Basic Books, 1983).

Special Features

An Evening Program for Every Season

FAMILIES TODAY COME IN ALL SHAPES, SIZES, AND MAKEUPS. THEY HAVE busy, heavily scheduled lives with only a limited time to spend together. Families are invited to come to the special programs in this chapter together. For the many parents who may work during the day—leaving little chance to participate with their little ones in storytimes—the evening specials are cherished opportunities not to be missed. These special feature programs are essential to successful public library children's program planning.

While it is easy to be intimidated by adults in a library program, presenters should look at those audience members as assistants, not adversaries. With adults in the room, enjoyment is heightened. Adults learn reading techniques, stories, finger plays, and songs. They recall favorite stories from their childhood and model becoming a lifelong library user. Whether they openly admit it or not, adults often enjoy a children's program as much as the children.

Advocates of all-age storytimes offer the following positive outcomes: [9]

- Adults can lend a hand in storytime. The activities, crafts, or stories can be more complex than those presented to a group composed only of children.
- Parents and caregivers can interact with one another, fostering a sense of community in the library.

- Parents can discuss the storytime activities with other parents outside of the library.
- Children see their caregivers as lifelong lovers of libraries and reading.
- The program attendance is larger than a single-aged offering.

The scope of materials that can be used in a family program is much wider than for any other storytime. For example, when adults join their children in the audience, the material presented can appeal to an adult sense of humor, whereas younger children may take the story literally. In some cases, repeating the same material—thereby capturing both audiences—is warranted. This type of program offers the presenter a unique and often satisfying opportunity to observe the interplay between the caregivers and the children.

One way to turn occasional library users into repeat customers is to offer highly participative family programs. These should contain a good mixture of books, movement, and novelty. Most of the programs are easy to advertise and market. Because of the preparation involved, they are designed to be once-a-year offerings. Repeating such "special" programs too often makes them less special, and attendance will suffer. Keep these programs special, talk them up, and then tuck them away for a few years.

The preparation for these specials is uniquely different for each one. However, the key to them all is the advertising done prior to the program's offering. Concentrate on marketing each family program throughout the library. Place fliers in the story room, in the meeting room, and at the circulation desk. Send a press release to local newspapers and hang posters around the community advertising these special events to the families. Remember to conduct registration to allow enough time to order or purchase any materials.

An Evening Program for Fall: Teddy Bear Party

As participants arrive, they should place a name tag on themselves and a name tag on their teddy bear. (Download pattern 4.1 at alaeditions.org/webextras). Having classical music playing in the background sets a nice tone. Tagging the stuffed animals helps in case one is left behind!

My name is:

My teddy bear's name is:

Have tables set up in a square with one place set for each registered child. While parents and families accompany their child, they will be asked to stand behind their child or children during the snack time. A teddy bear placemat can mark each child's seat (download pattern 4.2 at alaeditions .org/webextras). Remember to keep families together when siblings are registered. At each place have the pieces for the craft gathered in a baggie. Have containers of tacky glue spaced out on the waxed paper sheets. At craft time, remind the audience that the glue will need to be shared. They can use a toothpick to place the glue as instructed. If they finish their craft early they can color their place mat.

Sit in a circle on the floor with the children holding their bears. As you begin, introduce yourself and your bear's name. Invite each child to introduce themselves and their bear.

Tell-and-Draw Rhyme

"Teddy Bear Storytime" From *Chalk in Hand: The Draw and Tell Book* by Phyllis Noe Pflomm. Metuchen, NJ: Scarecrow Press, 1986.

- Download patterns 4.3 a, b, and c at alaeditions.org/webextras.

Book

A Pocket for Corduroy by Don Freeman. New York: Viking Press, 1978.

Action Rhyme

Sound recording: track 10, "Teddy Bear." *It's Toddler Time* by Carol Totsky Hammett. Long Branch, NJ: Kimbo Educational, 1982, compact disc.

Flannelboard: Bear Gets Dressed

See pages 97–98.

Action Rhyme

Sound recording: track 13, "I'm A Little Teapot." *Preschool Action Time: Activities and Finger Plays* by Carol Totsky Hammett. Long Branch, NJ: Kimbo Educational, 1988, compact disc.

Craft: Pom Pom Teddy Bear

- Glue the head (medium size) to the body (large size).
- Put glue on two of the small pom-poms. Press the pom-poms onto the body. Set them so the bear can sit without falling over.
- Glue the two arms onto the body.
- Glue on the muzzle (small pom-pom), then the two googly eyes.
- Glue on the black bead for your teddy bear's nose.
- Glue on the two ears (small pom-poms). Set them right up on the top of your teddy bear's head.
- To finish up your teddy bear, you can add tiny bows, small silk flowers, and other fancy items.
- Set the teddy bears out of the way to dry while the snack is served.

Refreshments

Iced tea or apple cider, Teddy Grahams (served in Dixie cups)

Take Home

- placemat
- name tags
- pom-pom teddy
- small bag of gummy bears tied with a bow to enjoy at home

Materials

- name tags
- small safety pins
- placemats (printed on colored paper)
- crayons
- chart paper
- marker (for tell-and-draw story)
- books
- 2 CDs and audio player
- flannelboard
- flannelboard pieces for "Bear Gets Dressed"
- 1½-inch pom-poms (body, 1 per child)
- 1-inch pom-poms (head, 1 per child)
- ⅝-inch pom-poms (legs, 2 per child)

- ½-inch pom-poms (arms, 2 per child)
- ⅜-inch pom-poms (ears, 2 per child)
- small black beads (1 per child)
- googly eyes (2 per child)
- tacky glue
- toothpicks
- wax paper (cut into quarter sheets for children to place glue on)
- tiny bows or small flowers and trim for teddy bears.
- plastic sandwich bags (prepacked with craft materials)
- ribbon
- iced tea or apple cider
- cups (for drinking)
- beverage napkins
- Dixie cups (for snack)
- Teddy Grahams (Chocolate or Honey), with extras to offer older or younger siblings who have "tagged along" to the program
  Important: Recognizing that the health and safety of children is of the utmost importance, the foods listed in this resource are free of the most common four food allergens: eggs, peanuts, tree nuts, and milk. Deviating from the brand name will not assure allergen safety. For more information, see http://snacksafely.com/snackguide.
- gummy bears

An Evening Program for Winter: It's a Parachute Party

As winter approaches, children and parents are in need of indoor play activities that are fun and educational. Playing parachute games encourages cooperative play. Children must share and take turns. Because of the novelty of a parachute, even normally reluctant children will get involved. Parachute games help children develop their sense of rhythm and aid in language skills, perceptual motor skills, and listening skills.

All that is needed for this program is an open space, a parachute, and balls or beanbags. If funds are not available for a parachute, a king-size flat sheet can be an inexpensive substitute. Selecting a parachute for your group depends upon the number of participants and the space available to play with the parachute. Parachutes are available in bright, colorful designs and come in various sizes, including: 6-foot, 12-foot, 20-foot, 24-foot, and 30-foot diameters. The smaller 6-foot parachutes are a bit too small for most groups. Amazon.com offers different sizes of parachutes starting at approximately $25 at the time of this publication.

Between twenty and thirty children and their accompanying adults can be directly involved around the perimeter of a 12-foot parachute. Parachute games are for all ages; however, you may need to modify each game for the age group that is involved. While not necessary, it is helpful to group children according to their ages. Conducting two 45-minute programs works well. The first offering would be for children ages 3 to 6 and the second for children ages 7 to 11.

When planning your party, safety needs to be the primary consideration:

- Encourage the children to space themselves around the parachute so that there are no large gaps. Have the adults interspersed among the children so as to best sustain the weight of anyone put on top of the parachute.
- Have the participants hold the parachute with both hands at all times. If there are not enough handles for every child to hold onto one, you may ask all the children to hold onto the edge rather than a handle.
- Remind the group to be considerate of others. They should not kick under the parachute and they should watch their elbows, to avoid injuries. Remind children to look where they are going when under the parachute.

The Internet is full of parachute games for children of all ages. Searching by age group will provide ideas that could be used in addition to the ones offered here. Several music CDs have been developed specifically for parachute play and can also be incorporated into your party. Two to consider are:

Plunkett, Michael. *Shakin' the Chute: Fitness with a Parachute*. Long Branch, NJ: Kimbo Educational, 2010, compact disc.

Stewart, Georgiana Liccione. *Playtime Parachute Fun*. Long Branch, NJ: Kimbo Educational, 1977, compact disc.

- The leader should be holding the parachute along with the participants. He needs to maintain vocal control over the group at all times. The chanting commands attention and clearly instructs the participants.
- [Leader Chant] Come on, everybody, and gather round, hold that parachute and shake it on down. Shake—shake—shake and stop. *Repeat several times.*
- [Leader Chant] Hey everybody, that was really good. Let's get moving. Don't you think we should? *Instruct participants to hold the parachute with their left hand and face right. Walk in a circle. Repeat going left and holding the parachute with right hands.* Sing *Ring Around the Rosie* as you circle. At the end of the song, all fall down.
- Next, invite a quarter of the children to sit in the middle of the parachute. They must be as close to center as possible. If the parachute has four colors, it is easy to invite all children holding red, blue, yellow, green, and so on. Repeat the activity until all children have had their turn "on" the parachute. Sing "Pop Goes the Weasel" as you walk in circles. Walkers are holding the parachute as taut as possible. On "Pop goes the weasel" everyone pulls the parachute tight and the children in the middle will get a bounce.

Return all participants to the perimeter of the parachute and recite "The Noble Duke of York," moving the parachute accordingly.

The Noble Duke of York, he had ten thousand men.
He marched them up to the top of the hill, *(all lift parachute up)*
And he marched them down again. *(parachute down)*
And he marched them to the left, *(walk to the left)*
And he marched them to the left, *(walk to the left)*
And he marched them to the right, *(walk to the right)*
And he marched them to the right, *(walk to the right)*
And he marched them up, *(lift parachute up)*

And he marched them down— (*parachute down*)
Oh, what a silly sight! (*shake the parachute really fast*)

Have the children lay the parachute on the floor. Invite them to sit on the parachute as you share the story:

> Barrett, Judi. *Cloudy with a Chance of Meatballs*. New York: Atheneum, 1978.

Return all participants to the outside of the parachute. Throw small and light softballs or beanbags onto the chute and shake the chute, popping the objects up in the air. Ask the children what the balls could represent from the story. ("*Meatballs*.") After shaking, ask the group to work together to get all of the balls off the chute without using their hands. The group will have to work together to guide the balls to one side of the chute. Ask a parent to collect all the balls and remove them from the floor.

Have the children lay the parachute on the floor. Invite them to sit on the parachute as you share one of the stories below.

> Bowdish, Lynea. *The Carousel Ride*. New York: Children's Press, 1998.
> Chorao, Kay. *Carousel Round and Round*. New York: Clarion Books, 1995.
> Crews, Donald. *Carousel*. New York: Greenwillow Books, 1982.
> Murphy, Stuart J. *Animals on Board*. New York: HarperCollins Publishers, 1998.

Again, by color perhaps, have about one-quarter of the children go on the parachute while it is on the floor and lie down with their heads in the center and their feet pointing toward the perimeter of the chute. The rest of the group will walk around the parachute and gradually go faster like a merry-go-round. Take turns.

Play the audio recording below. The group makes big waves by shaking the parachute up and down while music is playing. They should freeze when music stops. Some possible variations while making the big waves are: jumping up and down while shaking; holding the parachute behind instead of in front and shaking; or making waves back and forth instead of up and down.
Sound recording: track 5, "Rock and Roll Freeze Dance"

> *So Big: Activity Songs for Little Ones* by Hap Palmer. Topanga, CA: Hap-Pal Music, 1994. Sound Recording.

For a final activity, invite participants to sing these words to the tune of "If You're Happy and You Know It."

When the parachute goes up
Stomp your feet
When the parachute goes up
Stomp your feet
When the parachute is high
And floats up in the sky
When the parachute goes up
Stomp your feet.

. . . bend your knees
. . . wiggle your bottom
. . . lift one leg
. . . shout hooray
. . . shake your head

If time allows, invite the children to offer other activity selections to go into the song.

For the final activity, tell everyone that on "one" and "two," they should lift the parachute up high as a group, gathering as much air under the chute as possible. When you say "three," they must let go of the parachute; swiftly pull the parachute with both hands behind your back. This will end the program.

[Leader chant]
Raise your colors to the sky.
Count to three and watch them fly.
One—two—three!

An Evening Program for Spring: Cinco de Mayo

As participants arrive, have Mexican music playing and have chips, salsa, and napkins set out around the room. Fiesta lights, a cactus, colorful streamers, and sombreros are appropriate decorations.

When you are ready to begin, sit in a circle on the carpet.

Opening

Give a brief history of Cinco de Mayo:

> May 5th is a national holiday in Mexico. On May 5, 1862, a French army invaded Mexico and attempted to conquer it. In the city of Puebla, four thousand poorly trained and equipped Mexican soldiers defended their country against the invading French. They successfully defended their land and culture. Cinco de Mayo is a day that celebrates the culture of the Mexican people. Big parties (called *fiestas*) are held with food, music, dancing, and handicrafts.

Read (or Tell) Mexican folktales

Selection 1: "The Drovers Who Lost Their Feet"
or
Selection 2: "The Endless Tale"
From *Horse Hooves and Chicken Feet: Mexican Folktales* by Neil Philip. New York: Clarion Books, 2003.

Craft: Make Mexican Paper Flowers

- Make a stack of six pieces of tissue paper.
- Cut the stack so that it's 12 inches wide.
- Begin at the top and make 1-inch folds in the entire layer, accordion-fashion, to form a fan.
- Secure the center of the fan with a wire twist tie.
- Trim the ends with scissors. You can cut an arch shape for a regular round flower or use fancy scissors for ruffled edges.
- Bend the fan in half at the twist tie and separate each layer of tissue carefully, beginning with the outside and working your way in.
- Add a stem made from chenille stem or artificial foliage.

Perform the Mexican Hat Dance

Sound recording: track 13, "Mexican Hat Dance." *Action Songs for Preschoolers: A Treasury of Fun* by Georgiana Liccione Stewart. Long Branch, NJ: Kimbo Educational, 2003, compact disc.

Book

Fiesta Babies by Carmen Tafolla. Berkeley: Tricycle Press, 2010.

Materials

- red, white, and green tissue paper
- scissors (arched or fancy edged)
- twist ties
- green chenille stems
- green leaves
- chips and salsa
- napkins
- bowls
- audio CD and player

An Evening Program for Summer: Popsicles in the Park

During the summer, families are busy with outdoor activities from baseball, swimming, tennis, and on and on. This program takes the library where the families already are. The key to making this program successful is the research done in picking a time and place. When scheduling, consider the times families are out and about but available for a half hour to wind down from their other activity. For example, consider when the local pool closes or takes rest breaks. Ask to have the library scheduled into that time slot. Contact the city to see if a permit is required to perform on the closest playground (or recreation center, or pool property, or T-ball field). Assure that there is a table available. Advertise! (download pattern 4.4 at alaeditions.org/webextras) Since the world is not perfect, consider an alternate date or location in the event of rain.

You Are Invited To

Join our Children's Librarians for an evening of Stories and Sweet Treats!

Date:
Time:
Location:

We'll bring the stories and popsicles, you bring a blanket to sit on!

In the event of rain, join us on the Rain Date of:

Schedule another staff member to accompany you. For safety it is necessary to travel together. Additionally, serving the popsicles is a two-person job. One person can take the popsicles out of the cooler, cut the popsicles open, and pass them to the children. The other individual can circulate to pass out wipes and collect trash. It is also a perfect time to pass out storytime fliers. If your helper is a children's staff member, share the presentation. The first rhyme requires two voices and establishes with the audience the theme of the stories. It is fun for the children to try to guess what all the following stories will be about. Choose a partner that is willing to ham it up. This is an opportunity to find new library customers and engaging the adults is a necessity. Be silly, go over the top, laugh, and smile!

Be sure to purchase enough popsicles for a large crowd. Even adults will accept a popsicle on a hot summer day. The staff can enjoy any leftovers when you return to the library. Ask the Friends of the Library for help and purchase enough for seventy-five people.

Opening

pp. 6–7: "The Mummy." Hoberman, Mary Ann. *You Read to Me and I'll Read to You: Very Short Scary Stories to Read Together.* New York: Little, Brown and Company, 2007.

Read (or Tell)

Baby Rattlesnake by Te Ata. San Francisco, CA: Children's Book Press, 1989.
   - Take a maraca (or other stick instrument from your collection), and as the story is told make the rattling sound of baby rattlesnake's tail.

Magnet Story

Are You My Mother? by P. D. Eastman. New York distributed by Random House, 1960.
   - www.theteacherexpress.com/areyoumymother.html

Movement

Sound recording: track 8, "Princess Pat." *Crazy Gibberish: And Other Story Hour Stretches* by Naomi Baltuck. Hamden, CN: Linnet Books, 1993, compact disc.

Read (or Tell)

17 Things I'm Not Allowed to Do Anymore by Jenny Offill. New York: Schwartz & Wade Books, 2007.

Movement

Sound recording: track 21, "My Aunt Came Back." *Wee Sing Games, Games, Games* by Pamela Conn Beall. New York: Price Stern Sloan, 2006, compact disc.

Book

I Ain't Gonna Paint No More! by Karen Beaumont. Orlando, FL: Harcourt, 2005.

Flannelboard: Flack the Cat

See pages 34–35.

Refreshments

Serve popsicles.

Materials

- books
- maracas
- magnet board
- flannelboard
- audio CDs and player
- scissors
- hand wipes and/or napkins
- cooler
- popsicles
- garbage bag

NOTE

1. Margaret Read MacDonald, *Bookplay: 101 Creative Themes to Share with Young Children* (North Haven, CT: Library Professional Publications, 1995).

Baby and Me
Rhyme Sheets

Fall Session

The itsy-bitsy spider
Climbed up the waterspout. *(walk spider fingers up baby's arm)*
Down came the rain
And washed the spider out. *(tickle baby's arm)*
Out came the sun
And dried up all the rain. *(make circle over head and sway to rhythm)*
So the itsy-bitsy spider
Climbed up the spout again. *(walk fingers up arm)*

(Bounce baby on knees.)
Bouncing, bouncing on my knee.
Bouncing, bouncing on my knee.
Bouncing, bouncing on my knee.
Just Baby and me.
I'll swing you high and swing you low, *(lift baby and down)*
I'll hold you close, and I won't let go *(hug baby)*

(Clap baby's hands in rhythm.)
Pat-a-cake, pat-a-cake, baker's man,
Bake me a cake as fast as you can.
Roll it and pat it and mark it with a *B*, *(roll baby's hands and tickle belly)*
And put it in the oven for baby and me! *(clap baby's hands)*

(Tap the rhythm on baby's feet, alternating right and left foot.)
Cobbler, cobbler, mend my shoe.
Get it done by half past two.
Half past two is much too late.
Get it done by half past eight.

Round and round the garden, like a teddy bear,
    (gently trace finger in a circle around child's palm)
One step, two step, *(walk fingers up child's arm)*
Tickle you under there. *(tickle under chin, under arm, and on tummy)*

Twinkle, twinkle, little star,
How I wonder what you are.
Up above the world so high,
Like a diamond in the sky.
Twinkle, twinkle, little star,
How I wonder what you are.

(Put one hand under the opposite elbow and wave,
    alternating right and left arms.)
Skinnamarink a-dink a-dink,
Skinnamarink a-do, I love you.
Skinnamarink a-dink a-dink,
Skinnamarink a-do, I love you.
    (sign I love you: *point to yourself, cross fists over heart,*
    point to baby, and repeat with reverse hand)
I love you in the morning, and in the afternoon,
    (for morning, *make low circle using arms;*
    for afternoon, *move arms in front of body)*
I love you in the evening, underneath the moon.
    (for evening, *move arms over head)*
Skinnamarink a-dink a-dink,
Skinnamarink a-do, I love you.

Winter Session

The old gray cat is sleeping, sleeping, sleeping,
The old gray cat is sleeping in the house.
The little mice are creeping, creeping, creeping,
    (slowly walk fingers up and down baby's arms and legs)
The little mice are creeping in the house.

The old gray cat is creeping, creeping, creeping,
  (slowly walk fingers up and down baby's arms and legs)
The old gray cat is creeping in the house.
The little mice go scampering, scampering, scampering,
  (quickly walk fingers up and down baby's arms and legs)
The little mice go scampering in the house.

Oh, the noble Duke of York,
He had ten thousand men.
He marched them up to the top of the hill, *(bounce baby up on lap)*
And marched them down again. *(bounce baby down on lap)*
And when they're up, they're up! *(raise legs up)*
And when they're down, they're down. *(lower legs)*
And when they're only halfway up, *(raise legs halfway up)*
They're neither up nor down. *(quickly legs raise up and down)*

Oh, the noble Duke of York,
He had ten thousand men.
He marched them up to the top of the hill,
And marched them down again. *(bounce baby down on lap)*
He marched them to the left, *(gently tip baby to left)*
He marched them to the right. *(gently tip baby to right)*
He even marched them upside down—
  (roll baby onto chest as you roll backward)
Oh, what a silly sight!

Up, up in the sky like this, *(gently lift baby in the air)*
Down, down for a great big kiss. *(slowly bring baby down and kiss)*
Up like this, *(lift up)*
Down for a kiss. *(lower down)*
You're a special baby! *(hug and cuddle baby)*

These are Baby's fingers, *(tickle fingers)*
These are Baby's toes. *(tickle toes)*
This is Baby's tummy button, *(tickle belly)*
Round and round it goes!

(Touch baby's face as you say rhyme.)
Cheek, chin, cheek, chin,
Cheek, chin, NOSE!
Cheek, chin, cheek, chin,
Cheek, chin, TOES!
Cheek, chin, cheek, chin,
Cheek, chin, UP BABY GOES! *(lift baby up)*

(Bounce baby to rhythm.)
Rickety, rickety, rocking horse,
Over the fields we go.
Rickety, rickety, rocking horse,
Giddyup, giddyup,
Whoa! *(roll backward; baby falls to chest)*

Spring Session

Jack be nimble, (bounce baby on knees)
Jack be quick. (bounce baby on knees)
Jack jump over (lift baby up)
The candlestick.
Mix a pancake,
Stir a pancake, *(turn babies arms as if stirring bowl)*
Pop it in the pan. *(bounce baby)*
Fry the pancake, *(bounce your knees so baby bounces quickly)*
Toss the pancake, *(lift the baby)*
Catch it if you can! *(give baby hug)*

The baby in the cradle goes rock, rock, rock.
  (rock arms as if holding infant)
The clock on the dresser goes tick, tock, tock.
  (shake pointer finger back and forth)
The rain on the window goes pat, pat, pat.
  (tap fingers together)
Out comes the sun,
So we clap, clap, clap.
  (raise arms in a circle over head and clap three times)

(Tickle each of baby's toes in turn.)
This little piggy went to market.
This little piggy stayed at home.
This little piggy had roast beef.
This little piggy had none.
And this little piggy went
"Wee wee wee!" all the way home! *(run fingers up knee and tickle on* home)

(Lay baby on the back and bicycle the legs.)
Diddle, diddle, dumpling, my son John
Went to bed with his stockings on.
One shoe off, and one shoe on. *(tap bottom of baby's feet, alternating)*
Diddle, diddle, dumpling, my son John.
   (lay baby on the back and bicycle the legs)

Mother and Father and Uncle John *(bounce baby on knees)*
Went to town one by one. *(bounce on knees)*
Father fell off, *(lean baby to one side)*
Mother fell off, *(lean baby to other side)*
But Uncle John rode on and on. *(bounce baby sitting upright)*
Father fell off, *(lean baby to one side)*
Mother fell off, *(lean baby to other side)*
But Uncle John rode on and on and on! *(bounce baby faster)*

Summer Session

Ten little horses galloped into town. *(gallop baby)*
Five were black and five were brown. *(emphasize one hand, then the other)*
They galloped up, *(gallop baby up)*
They galloped down. *(gallop baby down)*
Then they galloped their way out of town. *(gallop quickly)*

This is the way the ladies ride—
Walk, walk, walk. *(bounce baby gently on lap)*
This is the way the gentlemen ride—
Trot, trot, trot. *(bounce baby slightly more)*

This is the way the children ride—
Gallopy-trot, gallopy-trot. *(bounce baby quickly)*
Gallopy, gallopy, gallopy, gallop! *(bounce baby more quickly)*
All fall off! *(catch baby in your arms as baby "falls" off)*

One little baby rocking in a tree. *(rock arms as if holding infant)*
Two little babies splashing in the sea. *(pretend to splash)*
Three little babies crawling on the floor. *(crawl fingers on floor)*
Four little babies banging on the door. *(pretend to knock)*
Five little babies playing hide-and-seek. *(cover baby's eyes)*
Keep your eyes closed now . . . until I say . . . PEEK! *(uncover eyes)*

(Touch baby's body parts and tickle lightly.)
Put your finger on your nose, on your nose,
Put your finger on your nose, on your nose.
Put your finger on your nose, and see if it grows.
Put your finger on your nose, on your nose.

Put your finger on your cheek, on your cheek,
Put your finger on your cheek, on your cheek.
Put your finger on your cheek, and leave it for a week.
Put your finger on your cheek, on your cheek.

Put your finger on your ear, on your ear,
Put your finger on your ear, on your ear.
Put your finger on your ear, and leave it for a year.
Put your finger on your ear, on your ear.

Put your finger in the air, in the air,
Put your finger in the air, in the air.
Put your finger in the air, and hold it right there.
Put your finger in the air, in the air.

Put your finger on your finger, on your finger,
Put your finger on your finger, on your finger.
Put your finger on your finger, and let it linger.
Put your finger on your finger, on your finger.

Toddling into Kindergarten
Sample Opening and Closing Sequences

Opening Sequence

(Jimbo is a jack-in-the-box puppet.)
Oh where, oh where is my friend Jimbo?
Where, oh where is my friend Jimbo?
Where, oh where is my friend Jimbo?
Where can Jimbo be?
POP! *(Jimbo dramatically pops out of his box.)*

(Talk to Jimbo to introduce the theme of the day's storytime. For example:)
Jimbo, do you see all the books in my basket today? They all make me feel
    cold because there is snow on the covers.

(or)

Jimbo, why are you holding a tissue in your hand? Do you have the
    sneezes? Really? Our stories today do too.

(in a singsong voice)
Hello to all my friends today.
Hello, hello, hi.
Hello to all my friends today.
Hello, hello, hi.

Let's clap *(clap, clap)*
And tap *(tap, tap)*
And clap again like that! *(clap, clap)*

Hello to all my friends today.
Hello, hello, hi.

(using your own voice)
Jimbo, would you like me to start with the story of ——?

Closing Sequence

SSSSShhhhhh. Can you hear that? What is it, Jimbo?
   (Pretend that Jimbo is whispering in your ear.)
Oh, no! Jimbo knows the clock on the wall says our storytime is through.
But come back next week and we'll have more storytime fun!

Take your little hands and go clap, clap, clap. *(clap, clap, clap)*
Take your little feet and go tap, tap, tap. *(tap, tap, tap*
Take your little hands and wave bye, bye, bye. *(Wave Jimbo's hand.)*
Jimbo and I will see you back here next week.

*(Sing final song, blowing bubbles between lines as possible. Alternately, play
   an appropriate sound recording. I used bubbles with babies and toddler
   groups but ended with the above Jimbo sequence with preschoolers.)*

There are bubbles in the air, in the air.
There are bubbles in the air, in the air.
There are bubbles in the air, there are bubbles everywhere.
There are bubbles in the air, in the air.

There are bubbles way up high, way up high.
There are bubbles way up high, way up high.
There are bubbles way up high, there are bubbles in the sky.
There are bubbles way up high, way up high.

There are bubbles way down low, way down low
There are bubbles way down low, way down low.
There are bubbles way down low, there's a bubble by your toe.
There are bubbles way down low, way down low.

There are bubbles in the air, in the air.
There are bubbles in the air, in the air.
There are bubbles in the air, there are bubbles everywhere.
There are bubbles in the air, in the air.

Wish List

Dear Friends and Colleagues,

The Children's Department is pleased to announce that we will be offering a book club for grades K–2. In our preparations we are searching for some items needed in the games and activities we have planned. We are also creating two prop stories to use with preschoolers. Please search your basements, attics, and garages for the listed items. Some of them would just require saving some containers for us. Please consider donating any of the following:

- dog water bowl
- dog rawhide bone
- pieces of 8½-by-11-inch cardboard
- baskets
- stuffed animal pig
- witch hat
- goldfish bowl (plastic)
- popcorn tub
- apple bushel basket
- clean margarine containers
- lids from plastic two-liter beverage bottles
- 2 buckets
- 2 sponges
- 2 yardsticks
- plastic jack-o'-lantern
- paper egg cartons
- clean washed bandana
- costume jewelry, high heels
- fancy hats
- sewing box
- 1- or 2-quart cooking pot

- magazines
- single mitten
- red foil Valentine box
- plastic or silk shamrock
- purple plastic Easter egg
- plastic or silk daisy (flower)
- small plastic sand pail
- small American flag
- "1st place" award ribbon
- red plastic apple
- orange plastic leaf
- turkey wishbone (washed and shellacked)
- Christmas tree ball ornament
- plastic fireman's hat
- stuffed animal puppy
- stuffed animal frog
- large gift wrap bow
- rubber duck
- tiaras
- empty copy paper boxes
- two button-down sweaters
- plastic sled

(continued)

Your donations are appreciated. Please note that we will be unable to return your donated items.

Please leave the items in_____'s mailbox
by _____!

Thank you as always,
The Children's Department

Young Readers
Parent Letter

Dear Caregivers of the Young Readers' Book Club,

The Young Readers' Book Club works in the same manner as an adult book club. The boys and girls come together after having the common experience of reading the same book at home. The program focuses on sharing ideas with others. In order to participate fully in the program, it is expected that every child has read or listened to the book being read to them, at least once, before arriving in the library at (time) on (day of the week).

My goals for the children are:

- Learning to think critically
- Learning to respect the opinions of others
- Learning to communicate clearly
- Improving their reading skills
- Developing an appreciation of stories; both real and pretend

I encourage you to read and enjoy these wonderful examples of children's literature along with your child. Exchanging ideas with you at home—before meeting with the group—will help build confidence levels of any reluctant participants.

My role is not that of a teacher. Instead, I will be acting as a moderator. I help the children stay on topic and encourage everyone to participate.

I hope your young reader enjoys this experience. Every week I look forward to talking about books with your child.

Sincerely,

P.S. Each week you will be able to check out the following week's Book Club selection, so please bring your library card with you!

Young Readers
Glass Jar Reminder to Parents

[John Smith]
[Main Street Library]

Next week, (date), our Young Readers' Book Club title centers on the theme of recycling. For our craft, each child will need to bring in **1 glass jar**. It can be a soda bottle, or a sauce or condiment jar. Please wash the glass with soapy water and remove any paper labels. Thank you for your cooperation!

bibliography

101 Dalmations and Friends. Burbank, CA: Walt Disney Records, 2008, compact disc.

25 Thunderous Favorites. Hauppauge, NY: SPJ Music, 2000, compact disc.

Alborough, Jez. *Can You Jump Like a Kangaroo?* Cambridge, MA: Candlewick Press, 1996.

———. *Hug.* Cambridge, MA: Candlewick Press, 2000.

Amazon Rain Forest: Enhanced With Music. Chadds Ford, PA: Creative Music Marketing. Distributed by Valley Cottage, NY: Eclipse Music Group, 1996, compact disc.

Anderson, Laurie Halse. *Thank You, Sarah: The Woman Who Saved Thanksgiving.* New York: Simon & Schuster Books for Young Readers, 2002.

Andreae, Giles. *Commotion in the Ocean.* Waukesha, WI: Little Tiger Press, 1998.

Animal Playground: Playful Tracks from Around the World. New York, NY: Putumayo World Music, 2007, compact disc.

Animal Rock. Burbank, CA: Disney/Walt Disney Records, 2001, compact disc.

Apperley, Dawn. *Good Night, Sleep Tight, Little Bunnies.* New York: Scholastic, 2002.

Araki, Mie. *Kitten's Big Adventure.* Orlando, FL: Gulliver Books/Harcourt, 2005.

Asch, Frank. *Bread and Honey.* New York: Dutton Children's Books, 1982.

———. *Water.* San Diego, CA: Harcourt Brace, 1995.

Ashman, Linda. *Babies on the Go.* San Diego, CA: Harcourt, 2003.

———. *Rub a Dub Sub.* San Diego, CA: Harcourt, 2003.

———. *Starry Safari.* Orlando, FL: Harcourt, 2005.

Asquith, Ros. *Babies.* New York: Simon & Schuster Books for Young Readers, 2003.

Ata, Te. *Baby Rattlesnake.* San Francisco, CA: Children's Book Press, 1989.

Auch, Mary Jane. *The Princess and the Pizza.* New York: Holiday House, 2002.

Augarde, Steve. *The New Yellow Bulldozer.* Brooklyn, NY: Ragged Bears, 2003.

Baker, Keith. *Big Fat Hen.* San Diego, CA: Harcourt Brace, 1994.

Baltuck, Naomi. *Crazy Gibberish: And Other Story Hour Stretches.* Hamden, CN: Linnet Books, 1993, compact disc.

Banks, Kate. *That's Papa's Way.* New York: Frances Foster Books, 2009.

Barber, Tiki. *Teammates.* New York: Simon & Schuster Books for Young Readers, 2006.

Barbour, Karen. *Little Nino's Pizzaria.* San Diego, CA: Harcourt Brace Jovanovich, 1987.

Barner, Bob. *Bugs! Bugs! Bugs!* San Francisco, CA: Chronicle Books, 1999.

Barney's Greatest Hits: The Early Years. Capitol Records, 2000, compact disc.

Barrett, Judi. *Cloudy with a Chance of Meatballs.* New York: Atheneum, 1978.

Barroux. *My Goldfish.* Grand Rapids, MI: Eerdmans Books for Young Readers, 2006.

Bartels, Joanie. *Morning Magic.* Van Nuys, CA: BMG Music, 1987, compact disc.

Barton, Byron. *Machines at Work.* New York: Crowell, 1987.

Bauer, Marion Dane. *In Like a Lion, Out Like a Lamb.* New York: Holiday House, 2011.

Beall, Pamela Conn. *Wee Sing Games, Games, Games.* New York: Price Stern Sloan, 2006, compact disc.

Beaumont, Karen. *I Ain't Gonna Paint No More!* Orlando, FL: Harcourt, 2005.

———. *Move Over Rover!* Orlando, FL: Harcourt, 2006.

Becker, Donny. *Sing Gymboree: 30 Favorite Songs, Fingerplays, and Movement Activities.* The Gymboree Corporation, 1991, compact disc.

Benton, Gail, and Trisha Waichulaitis. *Ready-to-Go Storytimes: Fingerplays, Scripts, Patterns, Music, and More.* New York: Neal Schuman, 2003.

Berkner, Laurie. *Victor Vito.* New York: Two Tomatoes, 1999, compact disc.

———. *Whaddaya Think of That?* New York: Two Tomatoes, 1997, compact disc.

Billy, Mr. *Big Pumpkin.* Doctors Orders Music, 2009, compact disc.

Blackstone, Stella. *Cleo's Colors.* Cambridge, MA: Barefoot Books, 2006.

Bowdish, Lynea. *The Carousel Ride.* New York: Children's Press, 1998.

Breen, Steve. *Stick.* New York: Dial Books for Young Readers, 2007.

Brenner, Barbara. *Good Morning, Garden.* Chanhassen, MN: NorthWord Press, 2004.

Brett, Jan. *The Mitten: A Ukrainian Folktale.* New York: Putnam, 1989.

Bridwell, Norman. *Clifford's First Easter.* New York: Scholastic, 1995.

Bright, Robert. *My Red Umbrella.* New York: William Morrow & Company, 1959.

Broach, Elise. *Snowflake Baby.* New York: Little, Brown & Company, 2011.

Brown, Margaret Wise. *Big Red Barn.* New York: Harper & Row, 1989.

———. *The Fish With a Deep Sea Smile: Stories and Poems for Reading to Young Children.* New York: E. P. Dutton & Co. 1938.

———. *Goodnight Moon.* New York: Harper & Row, 1947.

Brown, Ruth. *Ten Seeds.* New York: Knopf, 2001.

Browne, Anthony. *Willy the Dreamer.* Cambridge, MA: Candlewick Press, 1998.

Brownlow, Mike. *Bouncing Babies.* Brooklyn, NY: Ragged Bears, 2002.

Bruce, Lisa. *Grow Flower, Grow!* (Originally titled *Fran's Flower*) New York: Scholastic, 2001.

Buchman, Rachel. *Sing a Song of Seasons.* Cambridge, MA: Rounder Kids, 1997, compact disc.

Bunting, Eve. *Sing a Song of Piglets: A Calendar in Verse.* New York: Clarion Books, 2002.

Burns, Kate. *Jump like a Frog.* London: David & Charles Children's Books, 1999.

Burris, Priscilla. *Five Green and Speckled Frogs.* New York: Scholastic, 2002.

Butler, John. *Whose Nose and Toes?* New York: Viking, 2004.

Butterworth, Nick. *Jasper's Beanstalk.* New York: Bradbury Press ; Toronto: Maxwell Macmillan; Canada ; New York: Maxwell Macmillan International, 1993.

Cabrera, Jane. *Cat's Colors.* New York: Dial Books for Young Readers, 1997.

Campbell, Rod. *Dear Zoo.* New York: Four Winds Press, 1982.

Carle, Eric. *From Head to Toe.* New York: HarperCollins, 1997.

———. *Little Cloud.* New York: Philomel Books, 1996.

———. *Today Is Monday.* New York: Philomel Books, 1993.

———. *The Very Busy Spider.* New York: Philomel Books, 1984.

———. *The Very Hungry Caterpillar.* New York: Philomel Books. 1987.

Carlson, Nancy L. *How about a Hug?* New York: Viking, 2001.

Carlstrom, Nancy White. *Jesse Bear, What Will You Wear?* New York: Macmillan ; London: Collier Macmillan, 1986.

Carr, Jan. *Dappled Apples.* New York: Holiday House, 2001.

———. *Frozen Noses.* New York: Holiday House, 1999.

———. *Splish, Splash, Spring.* New York: Holiday House, 2001.

———. *Sweet Hearts.* New York: Holiday House, 2002.

Carter, Don. *Get to Work, Trucks!* Brookfield, CT: Roaring Brook Press, 2002.

Cedarmont Kid Singers. *100 Sing-Along-Songs for Kids.* Franklin, TN, 2007, compact disc.

Chalmers, Mary. *Easter Parade.* New York: Harper & Row, 1988.

Charlip, Remy. *Sleepytime Rhyme.* New York: Greenwillow Books, 1999.

A Child's Celebration of Song. Redway, CA: Music for Little People, 1992, compact disc.

Chitwood, Suzanne. *Wake Up, Big Barn!* New York: Scholastic, 2002.

Chodos-Irvine, Margaret. *Ella Sarah Gets Dressed.* San Diego, CA: Harcourt, 2003.

Chorao, Kay. *Carousel Round and Round.* New York: Clarion Books, 1995.

Christelow, Eileen. *Five Little Monkeys Bake a Birthday Cake.* Formerly titled *Don't Wake Up Mama.* New York: Clarion Books, 1992.

———. *Five Little Monkeys Jumping on the Bed.* New York: Clarion Books, 1989.

Church, Caroline Jayne. *Here Comes Easter!* New York: Cartwheel Books, 2010.

Cimarusti, Marie Torres. *Peek-a-Bloom.* New York: Dutton Children's Books, 2010.

———. *Peek-a-Moo.* New York: Dutton's Children's Books, 1998.

Cocca-Leffler, Maryanne. *One Heart: A Valentine Counting Book.* New York: Cartwheel Books, 2009.

Colandro, Lucille. *There Was an Old Lady Who Swallowed a Chick.* New York: Cartwheel Books, 2009.

Colborn, Mary Palenick. *Rainy Day Slug.* Seattle, WA: Sasquatch Books, 2000.

Corey, Shana. *Players in Pigtails.* New York: Scholastic Press, 2003.

Cousins, Lucy. *Hooray for Fish!* Cambridge, MA: Candlewick Press, 2005.

Cowley, Joy. *Mrs. Wishy-Washy's Farm.* New York: Philomel Books, 2003.

Crews, Donald. *Carousel.* New York: Greenwillow Books, 1982.

Cullen, Lynn. *Moi and Marie Antoinette.* New York: Bloomsbury Children's Books: Distributed to the trade by Holtzbrinck Publishers, 2006.

Czekaj, Jef. *Cat Secrets.* New York: Balzer & Bray, 2011.

Degan, Bruce. *Jamberry.* New York: Harper & Row, 1983.

Degman, Lori. *1 Zany Zoo.* New York: Simon & Schuster Books for Young Readers, 2010.

Denslow, Sharon Phillips. *In the Snow.* New York: Greenwillow Books, 2005.

DePaola, Tommie. *Strega Nona: An Old Tale.* Englewood Cliffs, NJ: Prentice Hall, 1975.

Diakité, Penda. *I Lost My Tooth in Africa.* New York: Scholastic Press, 2006.

Diaper Gym: Fun Activities for Babies on the Move. Long Branch, NJ: Kimbo Educational, 1985, compact disc.

Dines, Katherine. *Hunk-ta-bunk-ta Wiggle. Volume One: 12 Tunes for Toddlers.* Denver, CO: Hunk-Ta-Bunk-Ta Music, 2006, compact disc.

DiPucchio, Kelly. *Gilbert Goldfish Wants a Pet.* New York: Dial Books for Young Readers, 2011.

Dodd, Emma. *Dog's Colorful Day: A Messy Story about Colors and Counting.* New York: Dutton Children's Books, 2000.

———. *I Don't Want a Cool Cat!* New York: Little, Brown and Company, 2010.

———. *I Don't Want a Posh Dog!* New York: Little, Brown and Company, 2008.

———. *I Love Bugs!* New York: Holiday House, 2010.

Dodds, Dayle Ann. *Where's Pup?* New York: Dial Books for Young Readers, 2003.

Donaldson, Julia. *Room on the Broom.* New York: Dial Books for Young Readers, 2001.

Downey, Lynn. *The Flea's Sneeze.* New York: Holt, 2000.

Downing, Johnette. *Fins and Grins.* New Orleans, LA: Wiggle Worm Records, 2006, compact disc.

———. *Music Time.* New Orleans, LA: Wiggle Worm Records, 2005, compact disc.

Dragon Tunes. Los Angeles, CA: Kid Rhino, 2001, compact disc.

Durango, Julie. *Pest Fest.* New York: Simon & Schuster Books for Young Readers, 2007.

Eastman, P. D. *Are You My Mother?* New York: distributed by Random House. 1960.

Ehlert, Lois. *Boo to You!* New York: Beach Lane Books, 2009.

———. *Fish Eyes: A Book You Can Count On.* San Diego, CA: Harcourt Brace Jovanovich, 1990.

———. *Growing Vegetable Soup.* San Diego, CA: Harcourt Brace Jovanovich, 1987.

———. *Leaf Man.* Orlando, FL: Harcourt, 2005.

———. *Planting a Rainbow.* San Diego, CA: Harcourt Brace Jovanovich, 1988.

———. *Rrralph.* New York: Beach Lane Books, 2011.

———. *Snowballs.* San Diego, CA: Harcourt Brace, 1995.

———. *Top Cat.* San Diego, CA: Harcourt Brace, 1998.

Ellwand, David. *The Big Book of Beautiful Babies.* New York: Dutton Children's Books, 1995.

Ernst, Lisa Campbell. *Wake Up, It's Spring!* New York: HarperCollins, 2003.

Evans, Lezlie. *The Bunnies' Picnic.* New York: Hyperion Books for Children, 2007.

Fallon, Jimmy. *Snowball Fight.* New York: Dutton Children's Books, 2005.

Falwell, Cathryn. *Mystery Vine.* New York: Greenwillow Books, 2009.

———. *Turtle Splash! Countdown at the Pond.* New York: Greenwillow Books, 2001.

Faulkner, Keith. *The Wide-Mouthed Frog: A Pop-up Book.* New York: Dial Books for Young Readers, 1996.

Favorite Sing-a-Longs. Volumes 1–3. St. Laurent, Quebec, Canada: Madacy Entertainment Group, 2000, compact disc.

Feierabend, John Martin. *Frog in the Meadow: Music, Now I'm Two!* Chicago, IL: GIA Publications, 2000, compact disc.

———. *Ride Away on Your Horses: Music, Now I'm One!* Chicago, IL: GIA Publications, 2000, compact disc.

Feiffer, Jules. *Bark George.* New York: HarperCollins Publishers, 1999.

Finn, Isobel. *The Very Lazy Ladybug.* Wilton, CT: Tiger Tales, 1999.

Flather, Lisa. *Ten Silly Dogs: A Countdown Story.* New York: Orchard Books, 1999.

Fleming, Denise. *Barnyard Banter.* New York: Holt, 1994.

———. *The First Day of Winter.* New York: Henry Holt and Co., 2005.

———. *In the Small, Small Pond.* New York: Henry Holt, 1993.

———. *Lunch.* New York: Henry Holt, 1992.

———. *Mama Cat Has Three Kittens.* New York: Henry Holt, 1998.

———. *Pumpkin Eye.* New York: Henry Holt & Co., 2001.

Florian, Douglas. *Vegetable Garden.* San Diego, CA: Harcourt Brace Jovanovich, 1991.

Foley, Greg E. *Don't Worry Bear.* New York: Viking, 2008.

Ford, Miela. *What Color Was the Sky Today?* New York: Greenwillow Books, 1997.

Fox, Christyan. *Bathtime PiggyWiggy.* Brooklyn, NY: Handprint Books, 2001.

Fox, Mem. *Time for Bed.* San Diego, CA: Harcourt Bruce Jovanovich, 1993.

Freeman, Don. *A Pocket for Corduroy.* New York: Viking Press, 1978.

Gabriel, Ashala. *Night Night Toes: A Lift-the-Flap Story.* New York: Little Simon, 2002.

Galdone, Paul. *The Three Little Kittens.* New York: Clarion Books, 1986.

George, Kristine O'Connell. *One Mitten.* New York: Clarion Books, 2004.

George, Lindsey Barrett. *That Pup!* New York: Greenwillow Books, 2011.

Gershator, Phillis. *When It Starts to Snow.* New York: Henry Holt, 1998.

———. *Zzzng! Zzzng! Zzzng! A Yoruba Tale.* New York: Orchard Books, 1996.

Goldstone, Bruce. *The Beastly Feast.* New York: Henry Holt, 1998.

Goodman, Joan E. *Bernard's Bath.* Honesdale, PA: Boyds Mills Press, 1996.

Graham, Bob. *"Let's Get a Pup!" Said Kate.* Cambridge, MA: Candlewick Press, 2001.

Greenfield, Eloise. *Water, Water.* New York: HarperFestival, 1999.

——. *The Great Depression: American Music in the 30's.* New York: Columbia, 1993, compact disc.

Greenspun, Adele Aron. *Bunny and Me.* New York: Scholastic, 2000.

Greenstein, Elaine. *One Little Lamb.* New York: Viking, 2004.

——. *One Little Seed.* New York: Viking, 2004.

Greg & Steve. *Fun and Games: Learning to Play, Playing to Learn.* Acton, CA: Greg & Steve Productions, 2002, compact disc.

——. *Kids in Action.* Acton, CA: Greg & Steve Productions ; [S.1.]: distributed by Youngheart Music, 2000, compact disc.

Grover, David. *Caterpillar Butterfly: Songs to Help Kids Grow Wings.* West Stockbridge, MA: National Children's Music Project, 2005, compact disc.

Grubb, Lisa. *Happy Dog.* New York: Philomel Books, 2003.

Guthrie, Woody. *Woody Guthrie Sings Folk Songs.* Washington DC: Smithsonian/Folkways. Cambridge, MA: Rounder Records, 1989, compact disc.

Hall, Zoe. *It's Pumpkin Time!* New York: Scholastic, 1994.

——. *The Surprise Garden.* New York: Blue Sky Press, 1998.

Hammett, Carol Totsky. *It's Toddler Time.* Long Branch, NJ: Kimbo Educational, 1982, compact disc.

——. *Preschool Action Time: Activities and Finger Plays.* Long Branch, NJ: Kimbo Educational, 1988, compact disc.

——. *Toddlers on Parade: Musical Exercises for Infants and Toddlers.* Long Branch, NJ: Kimbo Educational, 1985, compact disc.

Harley, Bill. *Sitting Down to Eat.* Little Rock, AR: August House Little Folk, 1996.

Harper, Lee. *Snow, Snow, Snow.* New York: Simon & Schuster Books for Young Readers, 2009.

Hayles, Marsha. *Pajamas Anytime.* New York: G. P. Putnam's Sons, 2005.

Hayward, Linda. *Baker, Baker, Cookie Maker.* New York: Random House, 1998.

Hegner, Priscilla A. *Baby Games.* Long Branch, NJ: Kimbo Educational, 1987, compact disc.

——. *Teach a Toddler: Playful Songs for Learning.* Long Branch, NJ: Kimbo Educational, 1985, compact disc.

Helquist, Brett. *Bedtime for Bear.* New York: Harper, 2011.

Hendra, Sue. *Barry, the Fish with Fingers.* New York: Alfred A Knopf, 2010.

Henkes, Kevin. *Kitten's First Full Moon.* New York: Greenwillow Books, 2004.

——. *Little White Rabbit.* New York: Greenwillow Books, 2011.

——. *Oh!* New York: Greenwillow Books, 1999.

Hill, Eric. *Spot's First Easter.* New York: G. P. Putnam's Sons, 1988.

——. *Spot's First Picnic.* New York: G. P. Putnam's Sons, 1987.

——. *Spot Goes to the Farm.* New York: Putnam, 1987.

———. *Spot's Harvest.* New York: G. P. Putnam's Sons, 2010.

Hills, Ted. *Duck & Goose Find a Pumpkin.* New York: Schwartz & Wade Books, 2009.

Hoban, Julia. *Amy Loves the Snow.* New York: Harper & Row, 1989.

Hoberman, Mary Ann. *You Read to Me and I'll Read To You: Very Short Scary Stories to Read Together.* New York: Little, Brown and Company, 2007.

Hopkinson, Deborah. *Apples to Oregon: Being the (Slightly) True Narrative of How a Brave Pioneer Father Brought Apples, Peaches, Pears, Plums, Grapes, and Cherries (and Children) across the Plains.* New York: Atheneum Books for Young Readers, 2004.

Houston, Gloria. *My Great-Aunt Arizona.* New York: HarperCollins Publishers, 1992.

Hru, Dakari. *Tickle, Tickle.* Brookfield, CT: Roaring Brook Press, 2002.

Hubbell, Patricia. *My Crayons Talk.* New York: Henry Holt, 1996.

———. *Shaggy Dogs, Waggy Dogs.* Tarrytown, NY: Marshall Cavendish Children, 2011.

———. *Snow Happy.* New York: Tricycle Press, 2010.

Huff, Caroline. *Lulu's Busy Day.* New York: Walker, 2000.

Hulme, Joy N. *Easter Babies: A Springtime Counting Book.* New York: Sterling, 2010.

Huntington, Amy. *One Monday.* New York: Orchard Books, 2001.

Hurst, Carol Otis. *Rocks in His Head.* New York: Greenwillow Books, 2001.

Hutchins, Pat. *Good-night, Owl!* New York, Macmillan, 1972.

———. *We're Going on a Picnic.* New York: Greenwillow Books, 2002.

———. *The Wind Blew.* New York: Macmillan, 1974.

Intrater, Roberta Grobel. *Peek-a-Boo You.* New York: Scholastic, 2002.

Jackson, Alison. *I Know an Old Lady Who Swallowed a Pie.* New York: Dutton Children's Books, 1997.

Jarman, Julia. *Big Red Tub.* New York: Orchard Books, 2004.

Jarrett, Clare. *The Best Picnic Ever.* Cambridge, MA: Candlewick Press, 2004.

Jonas, Ann. *Splash.* New York: Greenwillow Books, 1995.

Joosse, Barbara M. *Dog Parade.* New York: Houghton Mifflin Harcourt Publishing Co, 2011.

———. *Snow Day.* New York: Clarion Books, 1995.

Kasza, Keiko. *Ready for Anything!* New York: G. P. Putnam's Sons, 2009.

Katz, Karen. *Counting Kisses.* New York: Margaret K. McElderry Books, 2001.

———. *Princess Baby.* New York: Schwartz & Wade Books, 2008.

Kay, Julia. *Gulliver Snip.* New York: Henry Holt and Company, 2008.

Keats, Ezra Jack. *Kitten for a Day.* New York: Four Winds Press, 1974.

———. *The Snowy Day.* New York: Viking Press, 1962.

Kellogg, Steven. *The Missing Mitten Mystery.* New York: Dial Books, 2000.

Kennedy, Jimmy. *The Teddy Bears' Picnic.* New York: Macmillan Publishing Company, 1989.

Kids Nursery Rhymes, Volume 1. United States: MasterSong, 2001, compact disc.

Kinsey-Warnock, Natalie. *Nora's Ark.* New York: HarperCollins, 2005.

Koontz, Robin Michal. *Creepy Crawly Colors: A Pop-Up Book.* New York: Little Simon, 2006.

Kopelke, Lisa. *Tissue, Please!* New York: Simon & Schuster Books for Young Readers, 2004.

Korda, Lerryn. *Millions of Snow.* Somerville, MA: Candlewick Press, 2007.

Kranz, Linda. *You Be You.* Lanham, MA: Taylor Trade Publishing, 2011.

Kunhardt, Edith. *Judy's Flower Bed.* New York: Golden Books, 2005.

Kuskin, Karla. *Under My Hood I Have a Hat.* New York: Laura Geringer Books, 2004.

Lawrence, John. *This Little Chick.* Cambridge, MA: Candlewick Press, 2002.

Lawrence, Michael. *Baby Loves.* New York: DK Publishing, 1999.

Learning Station. *Get Funky and Musical Fun with the Learning Station.* Melbourne, FL: Learning Station, 2003, compact disc.

———. *Where Is Thumbkin?* Long Branch, NJ: Kimbo Educational, 1996, compact disc.

Let's Dance. Burbank, CA: Walt Disney Records, 2010, compact disc.

The Lifesize Animal Counting Book. London, New York: Dorling Kindersley, 1994.

Lille, Patricia. *When This Box Is Full.* New York: Greenwillow Books, 1993.

Locker, Thomas. *Cloud Dance.* San Diego, CA: Silver Whistle/Harcourt, 2000.

Loesser, Frank. *I Love You! A Bushel & a Peck.* New York: HarperCollins, 2005.

London, Jonathon. *A Truck Goes Rattley-Bumpa.* New York: Henry Holt and Co., 2005.

Longview. *Deep in the Mountains.* Burlington, MA: Rounder Records, 2008, compact disc.

Lord, Cynthia. *Happy Birthday, Hamster.* New York: Scholastic Press, 2011.

Low, Alice. *Aunt Lucy Went to Buy a Hat.* New York: HarperCollins, 2004.

MacKinnon, Debbie. *Eye Spy Colors.* Watertown, MA: Charlesbridge, 1998.

MacLennon, Cathy. *Monkey Monkey Monkey.* London: Boxer, 2009.

Madison, Alan. *Letters from a Desperate Dog.* New York: Schwartz & Wade Books, 2007.

———. *Velma Gratch & the Way Cool Butterfly.* New York: Schwartz & Wade Books, 2007.

Mallat, Kathy. *Mama Love.* New York: Walker & Co., 2004.

Mantle, Ben. *Five Little Pumpkins.* Wilton, CT: Tiger Tales, 2009.

Martin, Bill. *Kitty Cat, Kitty Cat, Are You Waking Up?* Tarrytown, NY: Marshall Cavendish Children, 2008.

———. *Polar Bear, Polar Bear, What Do You Hear?* New York: Henry Holt, 1991.

Martin, Jacqueline Briggs. *Snowflake Bentley.* Boston: Houghton Mifflin, 1998.

Marzollo, Jean. *I Love You (A Rebus Poem).* New York: Scholastic, 2000.

McCue, Lisa. *Quiet Bunny's Many Colors.* New York: Sterling Publishing Company, 2010.

McCully, Emily Arnold. *Picnic.* New York: Harper Collins Publishers, 2003.

McDonnell, Flora. *I Love Animals.* Cambridge, MA: Candlewick Press, 1994.

McDonnell, Patrick. *Wag.* New York: Little, Brown Books for Young Readers, 2009.

McFarland, Lyn Rossiter. *Mouse Went Out to Get a Snack.* New York: Farrar Straus Giroux, 2005.

McGee, Marni. *Wake Up, Me!* New York: Simon & Schuster, 2002.

McGhee, Alison. *Making a Friend.* New York: Atheneum Books for Young Readers, 2011.

McGrath, Bob. *If You're Happy and You Know It . . . : Sing Along with Bob #1.* Teaneck, NJ: Bob's Kids Music, 2000, compact disc.

McGuirk, Leslie. *Tucker's Valentine.* Somerville, MA: Candlewick Press, 2010.

McMullan, Kate. *I'm Dirty.* New York: Joanna Cotler Books, 2006.

Meadows, Michelle. *Piggies in the Kitchen.* New York: Simon & Schuster Books for Young Readers, 2011.

Meltzer, Lynn. *The Construction Crew.* New York: Henry Holt & Co. LLC, 2011.

Miller, Margaret. *Boo Baby.* New York: Little Simon, 2001.

———. *What's on My Head?* New York: Little Simon, 2009.

Miller, Rick. *A Century of Baseball in Song.* United States: Cape Song, 2005, compact disc.

Miller, Virginia. *Ten Red Apples.* Cambridge, MA: Candlewick Press, 2002.

———. *Where Is Little Black Kitten?* Cambridge, MA: Candlewick Press, 2002.

Minor, Wendell. *Pumpkin Heads!* New York: Blue Sky Press, 2000.

Mitton, Tony. *Down by the Cool of the Pond.* New York: Orchard Books, 2001.

Mockford, Caroline. *Cleo and Caspar.* New York: Barefoot Books, 2001.

Moffatt, Judith. *Who Stole the Cookies?* New York: Grosset & Dunlap, 1996.

Monster Mash. Del Ray Beach, FL: Nesak International, 1995, compact disc.

More Silly Songs. Burbank, CA: Walt Disney Records, 1998, compact disc.

Mortimer, Anne. *Bunny's Easter Egg.* New York: Katherine Tegan Books, 2010.

———. *Pumpkin Cat.* New York: Katherine Tegan Books, 2011.

Moser, Lisa. *Perfect Soup.* New York: Random House, 2010.

Most, Bernard. *Cock-a-Doodle-Moo.* San Diego, CA: Harcourt Brace, 1996.

Moyer, Jeff. *Maxwell, the Dancing Dog: Songs for Children of All Ages.* Cleveland Hts, OH: Music from the Heart, 2001, compact disc.

Murphy, Mary. *Caterpillar's Wish.* New York: DK Publishing, 1999.

———. *How Kind.* Cambridge, MA: Candlewick Press, 2002.

———. *I Kissed the Baby!* Cambridge, MA: Candlewick Press, 2003.

———. *I Like It When . . .* San Diego, CA: Harcourt Brace, 1997.

Murphy, Stuart J. *Animals on Board.* New York: HarperCollins Publishers, 1998.

Na, Il Sung. *Snow Rabbit, Spring Rabbit: A Book of Changing Seasons.* New York: Alfred A Knopf, 2010.

Noonan, Julia. *Bath Day.* New York: Scholastic, 2000.

Numeroff, Laura Joffe. *If You Give a Cat a Cupcake.* New York: Laura Geringer Books, 2008.

———. *If You Give a Mouse a Cookie.* New York: Harper & Row, 1985.

Offill, Jenny. *17 Things I'm Not Allowed to Do Anymore.* New York: Schwartz & Wade Books, 2007.

OHora, Zachariah. *Stop Snoring, Bernard!* New York: Henry Holt and Company, 2011.

O'Keefe, Susan Heyboer. *Love Me, Love You.* Honesdale, PA: Boyds Mills Press, 2001.

Olson, K. C. *Construction Countdown.* New York: Henry Holt, 2004.

Olson, Margaret J. *Tell and Draw Stories.* Minneapolis, MN: Creative Storytime Press, 1986.

Palatini, Margie. *Piggie Pie!* New York: Clarion Books, 1995.

Palmer, Hap. *Peek-a-Boo: And Other Songs for Young Children.* Topanga, CA: Hap-Pal Music, 1997, compact disc.

———. *So Big: Activity Songs for Little Ones.* Topanga, CA: Hap-Pal Music, 1994, sound recording.

———. *Two Little Sounds: Fun with Phonics and Numbers.* Topanga, CA: Hap-Pal Music, 2003, compact disc.

———. *Walter the Waltzing Worm.* Freeport, NY: Activity Records, 1982, compact disc.

Parenteau, Shirley. *One Frog Sang.* Cambridge, MA: Candlewick Press, 2007.

Park, Linda Sue. *What Does Bunny See? A Book of Colors and Flowers.* New York: Clarion Books, 2005.

Patricelli, Leslie. *Be Quiet, Mike!* Somerville, MA: Candlewick Press, 2011.

———. *Tubby.* Somerville, MA: Candlewick Press, 2010.

Pedersen, Janet. *Houdini the Amazing Caterpillar.* New York: Clarion Books, 2008.

Peek, Merle. *Mary Wore Her Red Dress and Henry Wore His Green Sneakers.* New York: Clarion Books, 1985.

Pelham, David. *Sam's Sandwich.* New York: Dutton Children's Books, 1990.

Pellarin, Guglielmo. *French Music for Horn & Piano.* Detmold, Germany: Audite, 2011, compact disc.

Peters, Lisa Westberg. *We're Rabbits.* Orlando, FL: Harcourt, 2004.

Peters, Stephanie True. *Rumble Tum.* New York: Dutton Children's Books, 2009.

Peterson, Carole. *H.U.M. All Year Long: Highly Usable Music Kids Can Sing, Dance & Do.* [United States]: Macaroni Soup, 2003, compact disc.

———. *Sticky Bubble Gum and Other Tasty Tunes: Sing Along, Dance Along, Do Along.* [United States]: Macaroni Soup, 2002, compact disc.

———. *Tiny Tunes: Music for the Very Young Child.* Chicago, IL: Macaroni Soup, 2005, compact disc.

Pfister, Marcus. *Play with Rainbow Fish: A Deluxe Pop-up Book.* New York: North-South Books, 2009.

———. *The Rainbow Fish.* New York: North-South Books, 1992.

Pflomm, Phyllis Noe. *Chalk in Hand: The Draw and Tell Book.* Metuchen, NJ: Scarecrow Press, 1986.

Philip, Neil. *Horse Hooves and Chicken Feet: Mexican Folktales.* New York: Clarion Books, 2003.

Piggyback Songs: Singable Poems Set to Favorite Tunes. Long Branch, NJ: Kimbo, 1995, compact disc.

Plunkett, Michael. *Shakin' the Chute: Fitness with a Parachute.* Long Branch, NJ: Kimbo Educational, 2010, compact disc.

Raffi. *One Light, One Sun.* Willowdale, ON: Shoreline Records, 1985, distributed by Rounder Records (1996), compact disc.

———. *Singable Songs for the Very Young.* Cambridge, MA: Rounder, 1976, compact disc.

The Rainbow Fish: Come Swim with Me. Del Mar, CA: Genius Entertainment, 2003, compact disc.

Ransom, Candice F. *Tractor Day.* New York: Walker & Co.: Distributed to the trade by Holtzbrinck Publishers, 2007.

Rathmann, Peggy. *Goodnight, Gorilla.* New York: Putnam, 1994.

Redmond, E. S. *Felicity Floo Visits the Zoo.* New York: Candlewick Press, 2009.

Reiser, Lynn. *Ten Puppies.* New York: Greenwillow Books, 2003.

Richards, Laura. *Jiggle Joggle Jee!* New York: Greenwillow Books, 2001.

Riley, Linnea Asplind. *Mouse Mess.* New York: Blue Sky Press, 1997.

Robart, Rose. *The Cake That Mack Ate.* Boston, MA: Atlantic Monthly Press, 1986.

Rockwell, Anne F. *Apples and Pumpkins.* New York: Macmillan ; London: Collier Macmillan, 1989.

———. *Bumblebee, Bumblebee, Do You Know Me? A Garden Guessing Game.* New York: HarperCollins, 1999.

———. *The First Snowfall.* New York: Macmillan Publishing, 1987.

Root, Phyllis. *Soggy Saturday.* Cambridge, MA: Candlewick Press, 2001.

Rose, Deborah Lee. *All the Seasons of the Year.* New York: Abrams Books for Young Readers, 2010.

———. *Birthday Zoo.* Morton Grove, IL: Albert Whitman, 2002.

Rosenberry, Vera. *Who Is in the Garden?* New York: Holiday House, 2001.

Roth, Carol. *Ten Dirty Pigs; Ten Clean Pigs.* New York: North-South Books, 1999.

Rusackas, Francesca. *I Love You All Day Long.* New York: HarperCollins, 2003.

Rylant, Cynthia. *The Great Gracie Chase: Stop That Dog!* New York: Blue Sky Press, 2001.

Salerno, Steven. *Harry Hungry.* Orlando, FL: Harcourt Inc, 2009.

Sattler, Jennifer Gordon. *Sylvie.* New York: Random House, 2009.

Schertle, Alice. *All You Need for a Snowman.* San Diego, CA: Harcourt, 2002.

Schnitzer, Sue. *Wiggle and Whirl, Clap and Nap.* Boulder, CO: Weebee Music, 2005, compact disc.

Schoenherr, Ian. *Don't Spill the Beans.* New York: Greenwillow Books, 2010.

———. *Pip and Squeak.* New York: Greenwillow Books, 2007.

Schoonmaker, Elizabeth. *Square Cat.* New York: Alladin, 2011.

Schulman, Janet. *10 Easter Egg Hunters: A Holiday Counting Book.* New York: Alfred A. Knopf, 2010.

———. *Countdown to Spring: An Animal Counting Book.* New York: Alfred A. Knopf, 2002.

Segal, John. *Pirates Don't Take Baths.* New York: Philomel Books, 2011.

Seuling, Barbara. *Spring Song.* San Diego, CA: Harcourt Brace, 2001.

Seuss, Dr. *One Fish, Two Fish, Red Fish, Blue Fish.* New York: Beginner Books; distributed by Random House, 1960.

Sharon, Lois, and Bram. *One Elephant, Deux Éléphants.* Toronto: Elephant Records, 2002, compact disc.

Shaw, Charles Green. *It Looked Like Spilt Milk.* New York, NY: HarperCollins, 1947.

Shields, Gillian. *Dogfish.* New York: Atheneum Books for Young Readers, 2008.

Shulman, Lisa. *Old MacDonald Had a Woodshop.* New York: G. P. Putnam's Sons, 2002.

Siddals, Mary McKenna. *Millions of Snowflakes.* New York: Clarion Books, 1998.

Simply Christmas. London: Decca Music Group, 2003, compact disc.

Singin' & Groovin': 25 Best Sing-Along Songs. Redway, CA: Music for Little People. Distributed by Los Angeles, CA: Rhino Records, 2010, compact disc.

Slack, Michael. *Monkey Truck.* New York: Henry Holt, 2011.

Slobodkina, Esphyr. *Caps for Sale: A Tale of a Peddler, Some Monkeys and Their Monkey Business.* New York: W.R. Scott, 1947.

Smith, Danna. *Two at the Zoo.* New York: Clarion Books, 2009.

Songs for Wiggleworms. Chicago, IL: Old Town School of Folk Music, 2000, compact disc.

Sperring, Mark. *The Fairytale Cake.* New York: Scholastic, 2005.

Staake, Bob. *The Donut Chef.* New York: Golden Books, 2008.

Stewart, Georgiana Liccione. *Action Songs for Preschoolers: A Treasury of Fun.* Long Branch, NJ: Kimbo Educational, 2003, compact disc.

———. *Baby Face.* Long Branch, NJ: Kimbo Educational, 1983, compact disc.

———. *Bean Bag Rock & Roll.* Long Branch, NJ: Kimbo Educational, 2000, compact disc.

———. *Playtime Parachute Fun.* Long Branch, NJ: Kimbo Educational, 1977, compact disc.

Stickland, Paul. *Big Bug, Little Bug.* New York: Scholastic, 2010.

———. *One Bear, One Dog.* New York: Dutton Children's Books, 1997.

Stiegemeyer, Julie. *Seven Little Bunnies.* Tarrytown, NY: Marshall Cavendish, 2010.

Stockdale, Susan. *Fabulous Fishes.* Atlanta, GA: Peachtree, 2008.

Stoeke, Janet Morgan. *A Hat for Minerva Louise.* New York: Dutton Children's Books, 1994.

———. *Minerva Louise and the Red Truck.* New York: Dutton Children's Books, 2002.

Sturges, Philemon. *I Love Tools.* New York: HarperCollins, 2006.

Sunseri, MaryLee. *Baby-O!* Pacific Grove, CA: Piper Grove Music, 2005, compact disc.

Tafolla, Carmen. *Fiesta Babies.* Berkeley, CA: Tricycle Press, 2010.

Tafuri, Nancy. *Blue Goose.* New York: Simon & Schuster Books for Young Readers, 2008.

———. *The Busy Little Squirrel.* New York: Simon & Schuster Books for Young Readers, 2007.

———. *Five Little Chicks.* New York: Simon & Schuster Books for Young Readers, 2006.

———. *Have You Seen My Ducklings?* New York: Greenwillow Books, 1984.

———. *Silly Little Goose!* New York: Scholastic Press, 2001.

———. *Spots, Feathers, and Curly Tails.* New York: Greenwillow Books, 1988.

———. *This Is the Farmer.* New York: Greenwillow Books, 1994.

Taylor, Thomas. *The Loudest Roar.* New York: Arthur A. Levine Books, 2002.

That's Amore: Italian- American Favorites. Los Angeles, CA: Shout Factory, 2008, compact disc.

Thiam, Mor. *Back to Africa.* Montreal: Justin Time, 1999, compact disc.

Thomas, Jan. *A Birthday for Cow.* Orlando, FL: Harcourt Inc, 2008.

———. *Pumpkin Trouble.* New York: Harper, 2011.

Thomas, Patricia. *"Stand Back," Said the Elephant, "I'm Going to Sneeze!"* New York: Lothrop, Lee & Shepard Books, 1990.

Thompson, Kim Mitzo. *Birthday Party Songs.* [S.l.]: Twin Sisters, 2001, compact disc.

Thompson, Lauren. *Leap Back Home to Me.* New York: Margaret K. McElderry Books, 2010.

———. *Mouse's First Snow.* New York: Simon & Schuster Books for Young Readers, 2005.

———. *Wee Little Bunny.* New York: Simon & Schuster Books for Young Readers, 2010.

Tidholm, Anna-Clara. *Knock! Knock!* San Francisco, CA: Mackenzie Smiles, 2009.

Tierney, Fiona. *Lion's Lunch?* New York: Chicken House, 2010.

Tildes, Phyllis Limbacher. *Animals: Black and White.* Watertown, MA: Charlesbridge, 1996.

Titherington, Jeanne. *Pumpkin, Pumpkin.* New York: Greenwillow Books, 1986.

Urbanovic, Jackie. *Duck Soup.* New York: HarperCollins Publishers, 2008.

Valeri, Michele. *Little Ditties for Itty Bitties.* [S.l.]: Community Music, 2010, compact disc.

Van Allsburg, Chris. *Just a Dream.* Boston, MA: Houghton Mifflin, 1990.

Van Laan, Nancy. *Tickle Tum.* New York: Atheneum Books for Young Readers, 2001.

Vocal Essence Chorus. *Gratitude, Gravy & Garrison.* Orcas, WA: Clarion, 2010, compact disc.

Volkmann, Roy. *Curious Kittens.* New York: Doubleday Book for Young Readers, 2001.

Waber, Bernard. *Lyle, Lyle, Crocodile.* Boston, MA: Houghton Mifflin, 1965.

Wallace, Nancy Elizabeth. *Planting Seeds.* Tarrytown, NY: Marshall Cavendish, 2010.

Walsh, Ellen Stoll. *Hop Jump.* San Diego, CA: Harcourt Brace Jovanovich, 1993.

———. *Mouse Paint.* San Diego, CA: Harcourt Brace Jovanovich, 1989.

Walter, Virginia. *"Hi, Pizza Man!"* New York: Orchard Books, 1995.

Watson, Wendy. *Bedtime Bunnies.* New York: Clarion Books. 2010.

Weeks, Sarah. *Be Mine, Be Mine, Sweet Valentine.* New York: Laura Geringer Books, 2006.

———. *Bunny Fun.* Orlando, FL: Harcourt, 2008.

———. *Mrs. McNosh and the Great Big Squash.* New York: HarperFestival/Laura Geringer Book, 2000.

———. *Mrs. McNosh Hangs Up Her Wash.* New York: Harper Collins Publishers, 1998.

Wellington, Monica. *Apple Farmer Annie.* New York: Dutton Children's Books, 2001.

———. *Mr. Cookie Baker.* New York: Dutton Children's Books, 2006.

———. *Pizza at Sally's.* New York: Dutton Children's Books, 2006.

———. *Zinnia's Flower Garden.* New York: Dutton Children's Books, 2005.

Wells, Rosemary. *Red Boots.* Baby Max and Ruby series. New York: Viking, 2009.

Wheeler, Lisa. *Bubble Gum, Bubble Gum.* New York: Little, Brown and Company, 2004.

White, Linda. *Too Many Pumpkins.* New York: Holiday House, 1996.

Wiggles. *Racing to the Rainbow.* New York: Koch Records, 2007, compact disc.

Willems, Mo. *Pigs Make Me Sneeze! An Elephant & Piggie Book.* New York: Hyperion Books for Children, 2009.

Williams, Sue. *I Went Walking.* Cambridge, MA: Candlewick Press, 1994.

Williams, Vera. *Lucky Song.* New York: Greenwillow Books, 1997.

Wilson, Karma. *The Cow Loves Cookies.* New York ; Margaret K. McElderry Books, 2010.

Wilson-Max, Ken. *Lenny in the Garden.* London: Frances Lincoln Children's Books, 2009.

Winget, Susan. *Sam the Snowman.* New York: Harper Collins Children's Books, 2008.

Winnick, Karen B. *Barn Sneeze.* Honesdale, PA: Boyds Mills Press, 2002.

Wolff, Ashley. *When Lucy Goes Out Walking.* New York: Christy Ottaviano Books, 2009.

Wood, Audrey. *King Bidgood's in the Bathtub.* San Diego, CA: Harcourt Brace Jovanovich, 1985.

Wood, Don. *The Little Mouse, the Red Ripe Strawberry, and the Big Hungry Bear.* New York: Child's Play (International), 1984.

———. *Piggies.* San Diego, CA: Harcourt Brace Jovanovich, 1991.

Wright, Maureen. *Sneeze, Big Bear, Sneeze!* Tarrytown, NY: Marshall Cavendish Children, 2011.

———. *Sneezy the Snowman.* Tarrytown, NY: Marshall Cavendish Children, 2010.

Yolen, Jane. *Hoptoad.* San Diego, CA: Silver Whistle/ Harcourt, 2003.

———. *How Do Dinosaurs Love Their Cats?* New York: Blue Sky Press, 2010.

———. *How Do Dinosaurs Say Happy Birthday?* New York: The Blue Sky Press, 2011.

Ziefert, Harriet. *Snow Party.* Maplewood, NJ: Blue Apple Books, 2008.

Zion, Gene. *No Roses for Harry.* New York, Harper. 1958.

index